Do I Really Have to Teach Reading?

Content Comprehension, Grades 6–12

Cris Tovani

Stenhouse Publishers
Portland, Maine

Stenhouse Publishers
www.stenhouse.com

Credits

Page 8: From "The Demon in the Freezer" by Richard Preston, copyright © 2002 by Richard Preston. Reprinted with permission of Random House, Inc.

Page 30: From *Integrated Mathematics, Book* 2 by Rheta N. Rubenstein, Timothy V. Craine, and Thomas R. Butts. Copyright © 2002 by McDougal Littell, a division of Houghton Mifflin Company. All rights reserved. Reprinted by permission of McDougal Littell, a division of Houghton Mifflin Company.

Page 48: "Using Nonfiction Genres to Promote Science Practices" by Margaretha Ebbers, in *Language Arts.* Copyright © 2002 by the National Council of Teachers of English. Reprinted with permission.

Page 64: From Letters to the Editor. *Time.* October 28, 2002. Reprinted with permission.

Page 73: Jennifer Mooney, "Littleton Library Patron, 12, Pleads Guilty." *The Denver Post,* July 12, 2002. Reprinted with permission.

Page 76: Copyright © 2003 by BuddyT (http://alcoholism.about.com/), licensed to About Inc. Used by permission of About Inc., on the Web at http://www.about.com. All rights reserved.

Page 77: From *The Winter Room* by Gary Paulsen, copyright © 1989 by Gary Paulsen. Reprinted by permission of Orchard Books, an imprint of Scholastic, Inc.

Page 78: From *Glencoe Physical Science,* copyright © 2002, by Glencoe/McGraw-Hill. Reprinted with permission.

Page 120: "Did I Miss Anything?" from *I'll Be Right Back* by Tom Wayman, copyright © 1997. Reprinted with permission of Ontario Review Press.

Library of Congress Cataloging-in-Publication Data
Tovani, Cris.
    Do I really have to teach reading? : content comprehension, grades 6–12 / Cris Tovani.
    p. cm.
    Includes bibliographical references.
    ISBN 1-57110-376-7 (alk. paper)
    1. Content area reading. 2. Reading (Middle school) 3. Reading (Secondary) I. Title.
LB1050.455.T69 2004
428.4'071'2—dc22   2003065348

Published simultaneously in Canada by
Pembroke Publishers
538 Hood Road
Markham, Ontario L3R 3K9
Pembroke ISBN 1-55138-170-2

Manufactured in the United States of America on acid-free paper
10 09 08 07 06 05   9 8 7 6

For Pete, who helps me sing my life song

Contents

Acknowledgments　　　　　　　　　　　　　　　　　　　　　vi

1　Introduction: "I'm the Stupid Lady from Denver . . ."　　　1

2　The "So What?" of Reading Comprehension　　　　　11

3　Parallel Experiences: Tapping the Mother Lode　　　23

4　Real Rigor: Connecting Students with Accessible Text　　37

5　"Why Am I Reading This?"　　　　　　　　　　　　51

6　Holding Thinking to Remember and Reuse　　　　67

7　Group Work That Grows Understanding　　　　　89

8　"What Do I Do with All These Sticky Notes?"
　　Assessment That Drives Instruction　　　　　　　101

9　"Did I Miss Anything? Did I Miss Everything?"
　　Last Thoughts　　　　　　　　　　　　　　　　117

Appendix　　　　　　　　　　　　　　　　　　　　123
Double-Entry Diary
Comprehension Constructor with Connections Guide
"The Three Bears" Translation
Sample Text Set Guide Sheet
Instructional Purpose
My Answer Comprehension Constructor
Template for Reading Response Logs
Silent Reading Response Sheet
Weekly Calendar
Double-Strategy, Double-Entry Diary
Highlight and Revisit
Group Observation Form

Bibliography　　　　　　　　　　　　　　　　　　137

Acknowledgments

When I leave Colorado to do presentations, I am often asked how I do it. Teachers want to know how I can still be in the classroom, write books, and travel to work with other teachers. I tell them I can do what I do only if I give up something. I mention that I don't cook well. As a matter of fact, the best thing I make is reservations. I have messy cupboards and drawers—out of sight, out of mind. I don't iron. My garden is an embarrassment, and I buy Christmas cookies instead of making them. However, the real truth is I do what I do because:

My high school principal, Jeannine Brown, supports my work. She insulates me from tasks that take me away from teaching. She listens to my concerns and works very hard to accommodate instructional needs.

I have challenging students who share their thinking. Their questions propel me to discover why reading is so easy for some and so difficult for others.

My editor Brenda Power has a magic touch. Her ability to organize my random thoughts into a cohesive book astounds me. At Stenhouse, I can always depend on Philippa Stratton, Tom Seavey, and Martha Drury to answer questions and guide my work.

Stephanie Harvey encourages me to look outside my comfort zone and notice what's provocative in the field of education.

Ellin Keene challenges me to find a better way to teach adolescents how to read.

I learn from the visitors who observe my classroom and if I didn't have Sam Bennett and Chryse Hutchins naming the thinking and guiding the learning, I wouldn't be able to take the risks it requires to teach in front of my peers.

My colleagues at Smoky Hill High School push me to think. Their content expertise humbles me. Their willingness to open their doors reminds me how important it is to never stop learning.

For this particular book, Winter Caplanson, Sarah Malinoski, Ruth Shagoury, Lee Ann Spillane, and Suzanne Kaback read early drafts and provided direction for revision.

Rhiannon and Sara teach me that works in progress are worth the wait.

And the real truth is, none of this could happen without the support of my husband, Pete, who helps with the cooking and cleaning and car pooling. He encourages me and believes in me whenever I've lost faith. Without him none of this would be possible.

Last and most important, I have Carrie, who is the inspiration for everything I do.

1

Introduction:
"I'm the Stupid Lady
from Denver . . ."

The science textbook is hard for me to read. It has a lot of information with diagrams and pictures. All of these things are helpful to people who know the subject, but to me it is very confusing.

Evan, high school junior

It's a rainy Monday morning. I am sitting by an open window in a California high school science classroom, far away from my own students in Denver. I watch as students file in and fill the seats. I overhear a conversation between two girls:

"What are we doing today?"

"Remember? The stupid lady from Denver is coming to teach us about reading."

I realize they are talking about me, and the butterflies in my stomach flap a bit faster. I've been hired for the day to work at an alternative high school. My morning will consist of doing demonstration lessons in content-area classrooms, with the afternoon spent debriefing the lessons and sharing comprehension instruction with the teachers who are observing.

The stakes are high, with much expected of me. Teachers have been provided with substitutes so that they can come and watch the demonstrations. The principal's hope is that the teachers will learn how to help students be better readers of their content.

My first demonstration lesson is in this science classroom. The biology course is a graduation requirement, and the students taking the class are struggling readers who will most likely not be going to college. Much to my displeasure, I am to use the textbook chapter on viruses. I received the chapter earlier in the week, but had trouble getting through it. It is long, boring, and difficult to read.

It is challenging for me to plan these types of lessons, but I always request the actual textbook or reading materials in advance so that I can see the work from both the teachers' and the students' perspectives. I don't know the students, and I'm not an expert in the content. In this case, my ability to read the virus chapter closely resembles that of the students.

Sometimes not knowing the content well benefits me. My job is not to teach the content—that's the classroom teacher's job. My job is twofold. First, I am supposed to model a strategy that will help students become better readers of science. Second, I am supposed to model for the teachers a strategy that works not only with a specific chapter, but with all kinds of reading.

As I prepared for the lesson the week before my trip, I kept saying to myself, "Who cares? How does this stupid chapter on viruses affect my life?" I worried that if I couldn't get excited about it, how would I engage students I had never met? I needed to come up with a plan.

The plan didn't hit me until I was on the plane heading for my destination. I sat down next to a man who was invading my seat area. He was big and sweaty, and I didn't want to sit by him. But because the plane was full, I was stuck. We weren't in the air even fifteen minutes when the guy started sniffling and sneezing. As luck would have it, he let out a sneeze that sprayed all over me.

The sun from the window hit the mist of spit, and I could almost see the germs as they landed on me. Quickly, I covered my mouth and nose. I edged to the far side of my seat as questions began to flood my mind: Were this guy's germs going to recirculate throughout the plane? Did he have a cold, or was it allergies? Was a cold a virus? Could a virus be cured with antibiotics, or is that a bacterial infection? Is a virus alive? Is AIDS a virus? Do viruses mutate? Is that why we can't find a cure for AIDS and the common cold?

I pulled the "boring" textbook chapter on viruses out of my carry-on luggage. I started to read to find answers to my questions. Based on my own reading and thinking I began to formulate a plan for my demonstration lesson in the California classroom.

Now I stand by the windows, ready to begin as soon as the students are settled into their seats. A kid asks me, "Are you the sub?"

"No," I say. "I'm the stupid lady from Denver." The student looks at me and snickers. I head to the front of the room and begin adjusting the overhead projector. I introduce myself to the class and to the twenty teachers observing in the back of the room. Thanks to a science colleague in my high school whom I approached earlier that week, I am armed with some color transparencies of viruses she uses with her students. They were interesting to me, and I hoped they would generate some curiosity in these students. I begin showing them as a warm-up for the actual lesson.

More students straggle in as I run through the color overheads. One girl comes in and sits directly in front of me. She plops down, trying very hard to distract me, waving her arms and turning to chat with a student behind her. I keep moving through the transparencies. Most of the class seems interested.

After three or four minutes pass, this girl looks up, throws her arms in the air, and lets out a loud, exaggerated sigh. She drops her head to the desk and covers her face in her arms. I stop. Out of embarrassment, remembering the twenty teachers in the back who are wondering what I'll do next, I chuckle. She looks up. I stop and say, "So you're bored with viruses, too?"

"Yeah, who cares about stupid viruses? It's not like I'll ever need to know this stuff."

"I know what you mean. When your teacher sent me this chapter and told me I was supposed to teach a lesson on it, I did the same thing as you. I threw up my arms and let out a sigh. I didn't really care about it either. As a matter of fact, I didn't even want to read the chapter, but I had to, because I was going to be in front of a lot of people and I didn't want to look stupid. Because the chapter was hard and boring for me, I had to figure out a way to get through it."

The girl rolls her eyes, and I can see that she has something to say. I pause, and she jumps in. "There is no purpose in this science stuff. It's not like I'm going to be a scientist or anything."

"You've got a point. Maybe you're not going to be a scientist. But maybe there is another reason why you need to read this chapter and remember some of the information. Let me ask you a few questions. Do you need this class to graduate?"

"Yeah."

"Will your teacher give you a test on this chapter when you're finished studying it?"

"Yeah."

"Do you need to pass the chapter test to pass the class?"

"Yeah."

"Well, maybe what I'm about to show you will help you get through this boring text that you don't really care about in a way that will help you pass the test. That might help you pass the class so you can graduate."

By this time I have her attention. I begin telling the story of the man on the plane and how I always seem to sit by people who are sick and who sneeze on me. I share my questions and begin writing them on the board. I then show the class how my questions propel me through the chapter on viruses. I explain that asking questions is a strategy that I use to help me read uninteresting material.

I emphasize that the questions have to be questions that I really care about. I can't ask any old question—it has to be one that I truly am curious about. As my colleagues Stephanie Harvey and Anne Goudvis (2000) note in their book *Strategies That Work,* "A reader with no questions might just as well abandon the book" (p. 82).

We continue with the reading, and students begin to generate their own questions. At different points, we discuss how various types of information are conveyed through text, graphics, or figures—and how many of our questions are being addressed in the textbook. Before I know it, the bell rings.

The kids file out of the classroom, and a science teacher approaches me. She thanks me for the lesson and says, "Before you leave, I have a bone to pick with you. How can you say that viruses are boring?"

I smile and say, "Well, to a science teacher they might not be boring, but to an English teacher like me, viruses are definitely boring."

The science teacher replies, "You obviously haven't read all the fascinating articles about viruses. Do you know that some scientists think that viruses might hold the key to finding a cure for cancer?"

"No, I haven't read those articles. I had no idea that viruses could be so intriguing."

"Oh, yes, there are all kinds of great informational texts out there that are just fascinating to read."

I pause. Thinking that I have nothing to lose, I ask, "Then why aren't you using those articles with your students?"

My Roots of Learning About Comprehension

Fifteen years ago I began the quest to figure out how to help students think when they read. What was missing for those kids who could decode text but not comprehend it?

I was sure that comprehension could be taught, but I didn't know how. I was fortunate to become involved with a nonprofit staff development group based in Denver called the Public Education and Business Coalition (PEBC), a group of talented teachers who specialize in literacy staff development. When I became part of the group, it was led by Ellin Keene and Susan Zimmermann, co-authors of *Mosaic of Thought* (1997).

My colleagues from the PEBC, Stephanie Harvey and Anne Goudvis, have helped teachers throughout the country implement strategy instruction in grades K–8 through their book *Strategies That Work* (2000). Debbie Miller's *Reading with Meaning* (2002) has helped many primary grades teachers further refine their strategy instruction. Chryse Hutchins and Susan Zimmerman recently translated many strategies for use by parents in *Seven Keys to Comprehension* (2003). My own book, *I Read It, but I Don't Get It* (2000), is part of a growing number of texts on strategy instruction written for teachers of adolescents.

I remember the day Ellin introduced a body of research to the training team that we eventually called the proficient reader research. This research named certain strategies used by proficient readers of all ages. Ellin reasoned that if good readers used these strategies, perhaps we needed to be teaching them to struggling readers.

Since I first learned about the proficient reader research, my work has involved helping students and teachers learn how to become more aware of their thinking processes. I realize that if I want readers to reuse and remember the information they read, I have to help them know how to mark text. Highlighters, sticky notes, and different forms such as double-entry diaries and inner-voice sheets are tools that help students hold their thinking so that when they are reading difficult text, they can remember and reuse what they've read.

One critical concept embraced by both researchers and literacy specialists is that learning to read doesn't end in the elementary grades. Reading becomes more complex as students move into middle and high schools, and teachers need to help students understand difficult text. This may mean that teachers need to develop new strategies and skills for helping students. As Gerald Duffy (2002) writes, "We must continue to battle the public's long-held belief that literacy is a trivial matter of learning to decode the squiggles on the page, and that teaching itself is a relatively routine and one-dimensional task that any intelligent college graduate can do" (p. 348).

My work with the PEBC has taught me the importance of noticing what good readers do when they are constructing meaning. Good readers monitor their comprehension. They know when the text is making sense and when it isn't. They recognize signals that indicate when they are under-

Thinking Strategies Used by Proficient Readers and Writers

A strategy is an intentional plan that is flexible and can be adapted to meet the demands of the situation. Strategies give readers options for thinking about text when reading words alone doesn't produce meaning.

Good readers and writers monitor their understanding as they read. They recognize when the text is making sense and when it isn't. Some of the strategies good readers and writers use include the following:

1. Activating background knowledge and making connections between new and known information
2. Self-questioning the text to clarify ambiguity and deepen understanding.
3. Drawing inferences from the text using background knowledge and clues from the text.
4. Determining importance in text to separate details from main ideas.
5. Employing fix-up strategies to repair confusion.
6. Using sensory images to enhance comprehension and visualize reading.
7. Synthesizing and extending thinking.

Adapted from Pearson et al. 1992

standing what they are reading, and when they are confused. Good readers separate themselves from struggling readers when they recognize that they are confused and then do something to repair meaning. Good readers use "fix-up" strategies, which can be taught to readers at any age. They are useful with many different types of text structures and enable readers to monitor their comprehension. See the list on the next page generated by students who noticed what they did to help themselves when they became confused.

Teaching a few strategies well is a key aspect of my work. Rather than a large grab bag of gimmicks and techniques, I find myself returning to these core skills with students and teachers. I would rather my students master a few core skills than be exposed to so many strategies in a short period of time that they don't master any of them. Pearson (Pearson et al. 1992), too, makes the case for fewer strategies:

Currently, most reading curricula contain too many skills to teach. Pressured by so much to cover in so little time, teachers go quickly over everything, which leaves no time to teach anything very well. Everyone involved—teachers, students, parents—would benefit from a leaner, meaner comprehension curriculum composed of a handful of key strategies taught well and frequently applied to real texts. (pp. 188–189)

Although this model of teaching a few strategies well may be simple, it is not necessarily easy to implement—especially in middle and high schools, where teachers face increasing pressure to tackle a seemingly infinite amount of content within a finite amount of time.

Understanding Content Teaching

I have continued my full-time work as a teacher at Smoky Hill High School in Aurora, Colorado. But my responsibilities shifted beginning in 2001 to include more time with content teachers in my school. I now spend the morning working with three classes of students. Two classes are reading workshop, a course designed for students in grades 9–11 who struggle with reading. These students are identified by my colleagues as needing extra support, or by low test scores. I also have one section of English for college-bound juniors and seniors. These are high-achieving students who want additional strategies for meeting the demands of required college reading.

In the afternoons I work with colleagues from throughout the building in all disciplines who want to learn more about helping their students understand the difficult texts they encounter in classes such as math, science, and social studies. Teachers volunteer to work with me, and we develop lessons together, meet in seminar groups, and observe each other teach.

In addition to my full-time work, I often travel to middle and high schools across the country to help teachers understand and instruct students in comprehension strategies. Many teachers from other middle and high schools also trek to my classroom in Aurora to observe my work with students. More and more of my instruction with

---

Fix-Up Strategies

A "fix-up" strategy is any strategy used by a reader to help get unstuck when the text becomes confusing.

Make a connection between the text and the following:
>   your life
>   your knowledge of the world
>   another text.

Make a prediction.

Stop and think about what you have already read.

Ask yourself a question and try to answer it.

Reflect in writing about what you have read.

Visualize.

Use print conventions.

Retell what you've read.

Reread.

Notice patterns in text structure.

Adjust your reading rate: slow down or speed up.

Adapted from Tovani 2000.

students at my high school and with teachers nationally is in the content areas, because teachers outside of English classrooms are being called upon to assist struggling readers throughout the day.

I understand why content-area teachers are resistant to these calls to teach reading. Who has the time for it, when new content requirements are being added all the time through state and national standards? Few, if any, content teachers chose the profession because they wanted to be reading teachers, as Donna Ogle says:

> *Many middle and high school teachers think of themselves as content experts. When I started teaching, I thought of myself as a historian. I wanted to teach history, and I really didn't think much about how students learn. I always focused on content. A lot of secondary teachers enter the field because of their passion for what they are teaching. It's an unusual teacher who comes into secondary education wanting to teach students how to learn. Yet, if we're going to be good teachers, that's really essential. (in D'Arcangelo 2002, p. 13)*

Instead of thinking of this work as teaching "content-area reading" or "reading at the secondary level," I think of it as teaching students how to remember and reuse the information we ask them to read. Smoky Hill High School teachers don't see ourselves as reborn reading teachers. We are simply trying to help kids get the skills they need to understand and learn about the content we as teachers care passionately about, whether it is the roots of viral infections or the causes of wars in the Middle East.

For example, my colleagues Amy Krza, a biology teacher, and Ann Meisel, an English teacher, recently collaborated to find ways to link the reading content in their classrooms to help students become more adept at understanding science writing. Ann gathered a number of short texts from fiction and nonfiction with a science focus. Amy and Ann then worked with me to develop some simple lessons using comprehension strategies to help students become better readers of the textbook.

Instead of starting with a deadly dull excerpt from a science textbook to introduce students to viruses, they used the first four paragraphs from the essay "The Demon in the Freezer" by Richard Preston, which was originally published in *The New Yorker.* (See Figure 1.1.)

The opening four paragraphs grip readers with a grotesque description of the effects of smallpox on the human body. Amy and Ann had students highlight text in yellow with scientific terms they didn't understand. They then had them mark passages where the terms were defined later in the article. This activity helped students learn to slow down and look for definitions of unfamiliar terms, a useful strategy for reading any textbook.

Figure 1.1 "The Demon in the Freezer" by Richard Preston

The smallpox virus first became entangled with the human species somewhere between three thousand and twelve thousand years ago—possibly in Egypt at the time of the Pharaohs. Somewhere on earth at roughly that time, the virus jumped out of an unknown animal into its first human victim, and began to spread. Viruses are parasites that multiply inside the cells of their hosts, and they are the smallest life forms. Smallpox developed a deep affinity for human beings. It is thought to have killed more people than any other infectious disease, including the Black Death of the Middle Ages. It was declared eradicated from the human species in 1979, after a twelve-year effort by a team of doctors and health workers from the World Health Organization. Smallpox now exists only in laboratories.

Smallpox is explosively contagious, and it travels through the air. Virus particles in the mouth become airborne when the host talks. If you inhale a single particle of smallpox, you can come down with the disease. After you've been infected, there is a typical incubation period of ten days. During that time, you feel normal. Then the illness hits with a spike of fever, a backache, and vomiting, and a bit later tiny red spots appear all over the body. The spots turn into blisters, called pustules, and the pustules enlarge, filling with pressurized opalescent pus. The eruption of pustules is sometimes called the splitting of the dermis. The skin doesn't break, but splits horizontally, tearing away from its underlayers. The pustules become hard, bloated sacs the size of peas, encasing the body with pus, and the skin resembles a cobbled stone street.

The pain of the splitting is extraordinary. People lose the ability to speak, and their eyes can squeeze shut with pustules, but they remain alert. Death comes with a breathing arrest or a heart attack or shock or an immune-system storm, though exactly how smallpox kills a person is not known. There are many mysteries about the smallpox virus. Since the seventeenth century, doctors have understood that if the pustules merge into sheets across the body the victim will usually die: the virus has split the whole skin. If the victim survives, the pustules turn into scabs and fall off, leaving scars. This is known as ordinary smallpox.

Some people develop extreme smallpox, which is loosely called black pox. Doctors separate black pox into two forms—flat smallpox and hemorrhagic smallpox. In a case of flat smallpox, the skin remains smooth and doesn't pustulate, but it darkens until it looks charred, and it can slip off the body in sheets. In hemorrhagic smallpox, black, unclotted blood oozes or runs from the mouth and other body orifices. Black pox is close to a hundred per cent fatal. If any sign of it appears in the body, the victim will almost certainly die. In the bloody cases, the virus destroys the linings of the throat, the stomach, the intestines, the rectum, and the vagina, and these membranes disintegrate. Fatal smallpox can destroy the body's entire skin—both the exterior skin and the interior skin that lines the passages of the body. (p. 23)

In another activity with a different class, Amy and Ann had students in small groups mark images from each of the four paragraphs, and then draw a picture for each paragraph to visualize the effects of the smallpox virus. Students then reread the passages to verify the accuracy of their drawing. Visualizing is an important "fix-up" strategy for comprehending text that Amy and Ann want their students to develop while reading any text, whether it's science based or literary.

No Easy Answers

You won't find many quick fixes in this book for content teachers who want to help students delve deeper into texts. Often high school teachers are being told they must teach comprehension strategies, using worksheets or copied guides, or they are being handed specific programs and workbooks that are supposed to do this work for them. We are promised that if the program directions are followed closely, our students will learn how to read. Almost daily, my school mailbox is inundated with glitzy ads for expensive materials that promise to leave no teenager behind when it comes to understanding what they read.

Realistic teachers know it's not that simple. It is even tempting to get caught up in the hype about strategy instruction, believing that sticky notes and highlighters alone will help students become better readers.

But teaching strategies for the sake of teaching strategies isn't the goal. Being able to make connections or ask questions or visualize isn't what matters most. The only reason to teach kids how to be strategic readers is to help them become more thoughtful about their reading.

Meaning doesn't arrive because we have highlighted text or used sticky notes or written the right words on a comprehension worksheet. Meaning arrives because we are purposefully engaged in thinking while we read.

2

The "So What?" of Reading Comprehension

It really isn't hard to avoid reading—you just ask someone what it means, or wait for the teacher to explain it.

Lisa, high school senior

Recently a student named Erin helped me reconsider my beliefs about why comprehension strategies are important to learn in any discipline. It was late in the evening, after a full day of teaching and working with colleagues. I had given two classes of my students a copy of Sandra Cisneros's essay "Salvador, Late or Early" (1992). This short, difficult text is hard for readers of any age to grasp upon the first reading. I distributed copies with blank sticky notes, asking students to write two or three different connections they made to the essay.

As I was sitting at my desk reading what felt like thousands of yellow sticky notes with students' personal connections written on them, I couldn't help but feel I was wasting my time. I don't think I had ever read more banal responses—words that in no way reflected the depth of the essay or thinking that students would need to understand it.

I was getting nervous and feeling stressed. In the morning twenty teachers from across the country would descend upon my room to watch what was supposed to be exemplary strategy instruction. No way could I let them see these student connections and present them as any sort of effective reading instruction.

I was also worried about this student in my class named Erin. Erin was a brat. I could just imagine a student sharing one of these connections with the whole class, and then having Erin respond in her usual way. She had a horrible habit of shutting down other people's thinking. When someone said something she didn't think was interesting, she'd say in the most obnoxious tone possible, "So what?" The sarcasm in her voice was deadly.

What Are Double-Entry Diaries?

A double-entry diary is an "access tool" that students can use to hold their thinking. Like sticky notes or highlighting text, access tools help students slow down as they read and begin to track their thinking. Here's how to do a double-entry diary:

1. Ask students to divide a piece of notebook paper in half. The fold should be lengthwise, or "like a hot dog bun."

2. On the left-hand column of the page, students copy directly from the text. They might write quotes or individual words. Students can also write a summary of what they have read. The writing on the left-hand side represents literal information from the text.

3. On the right-hand column of the page, students share their thinking about the word, sentence, or summary that they wrote on the left-hand side. The writing on the right-hand side represents inferential and critical thinking.

4. Teachers choose how students will structure their thinking, based on what they ask for in the right-hand column (i.e., questions, connections, visualizing information).

5. Students choose what text they will use to apply the strategy or strategies chosen by the teacher as a focus.

I was stuck. Should I let the visitors see the real "us"? Should I create an errand for Erin so she wouldn't be in the room? I decided that I'd explain to the visitors beforehand about Erin. They would understand—we all have Erins in our classrooms. Perhaps explaining to the teachers what I had done to "help" Erin respond more positively would let them see that I too have problems with students, and work on them continually.

I had spoken to Erin privately about her rude comments, and I had spoken to her in front of her peers. I had even threatened to send her to the dean of discipline. Nothing worked. She had no desire to control her language and attitude. Every day I had to deal with whatever she threw my way.

I went back to reading the inane comments written on the stickies. After the fiftieth insipid connection, I had had it. Who could blame Erin when she said, "So what?" to any of these responses? Yeah, so what if this story reminds you of a tree? Yeah, so what if this piece reminds you of a tin cup? I couldn't take it anymore.

And then it struck me. Maybe I should be the one saying, "So what?" The time had come to ask that question about this assignment. How had strategy instruction helped these students understand Cisneros's writing? My students had followed my directions to the letter. They had done just what I had asked them to do.

It wasn't their fault that they were making stupid connections. It was mine, because I hadn't showed them how a meaningful connection could deepen their understanding of the text.

I decided to beat Erin at her own game. The next day in front of the visitors and the class I would share some connections students had written as part of the previous day's work.

The next morning I explained to my students that although they had done just what I had wanted them to do, we needed to go further. We couldn't stop here. I created a double-entry diary as a comprehension aid that would give students a place to hold their thinking and possibly force them to go deeper into the piece (see Figure 2.1). A blank copy of the double-entry diary form is in the appendix.

As the twenty teachers sat at the edge of the room and watched, I put a transparency of the double-entry diary on the overhead with a few examples from my

Figure 2.1 Double-Entry Diary Form

Double-Entry Diary	
Quote or description from a scene in the reading	**Record of the strategy being taught**
	For example: *I'm wondering . . .* *This reminds me of . . .* *I'm confused and this is how I got* *unstuck . . .* *The most important part is . . .* *My thinking has changed in this way . . .* *I'm picturing . . .* *I'm inferring . . .*

Remember: Don't ask students to respond to one quote in seven different ways. The ideas in the right column are options that the reader or teacher chooses.

reading. I wrote a connection to the story on the left-hand side, then said, "Now, to complete the double-entry diary you are going to have to think about your connection and ask yourself a question. I want you to reread what you wrote and pretend that Erin has sneaked up behind you and read your connection. She then asks you the very important question, 'So what?'" (See Figure 2.2.)

I tried to imitate Erin's sarcasm, complete with head tilt and curling lip. I must have done a pretty good job, because everyone knew exactly what I meant. I looked at Erin; she looked at me. She nodded her head and started writing. Erin finally got it too. Never again did she use the words "So what?" in the same fashion. She continued to ask the question, but from then on, the way she said the words encouraged thought instead of shutting her classmates down.

As students were filling out the diary, I began to circulate. I went to Anthony first. Anthony wrote that his connection was that he had a baby brother just like the boy in the story. "That's great, Anthony," I said. I continued gently, "I know you love your baby brother very much—but so what? How does that help you understand the story better?"

A bit disgusted, Anthony looked up and said, "Do you know how much work a baby is?"

"Well, yes, Anthony. Babies are a lot of work, but I still don't see the connection."

Figure 2.2 "So What?" Double-Entry Diary

Connection to the text	So what?
1.	1.
2.	2.
3.	3.
4.	4.

A little light went on, and Anthony paused for a moment. Then he replied, "Maybe: even though Salvador is just a kid himself, he is having to help his mom with the baby, just like I have to help my mom. Salvador's mom isn't being mean to him. Salvador's mom really needs and depends on him, just like my mom depends on me."

"How does that connection help you understand the story better?" I probed.

"At first," he said, "I thought the mom was being abusive because she was making Salvador take care of all the brothers and the baby. Now, I see that he is very important to his family. But I wonder, where is the dad? Maybe there is no dad, and that's another reason why Salvador has to do so much. He's the man of the house."

I smiled. Anthony had not only made a connection to his personal life, but had used that connection to understand the text. When he took his connection back to the text, he went deeper into the story. Anthony asked a question that ultimately allowed him to infer meaning. He went beyond the words on the page and drew a fabulous connection. (Figure 2.3 shows a thoughtful example by another student.)

I headed for Jo Anna's desk. She was chatting with a neighbor, her notes on the "So What?" double-entry diary sitting on the edge of her desk. I asked to see her sheet. She proudly handed it to me. All the columns were filled out, but once again her responses were superficial.

"Pick a line, Jo Anna, that you want to share with me."

Figure 2.3 "So What?" Student Sample

Connection	So What...
when my raggy ann doll got her head ripped off and I was so sad and hurt.	I can picture what salvador looks like all ~~better off need~~ skinny with out food.

Connection	So What...
a box of crayons are in order by color and all neat and organized.	I think it is parralelism between the box of crayons being all nice a neat and his past that could of be good til something happend. Salvador dropped his

Connection	So What...
✗	box of crayons on the street so that could show the relationship to what is happening now with him being hurt.

Connection	So What...
	I think salvador is being compared to being a catapillar then he turns into a butterfly.

Jo Anna read one of her connections to me—she used a tin cup when she went camping just like the boy in the story did when he ate his morning cereal. Her "So what?" wasn't really what I had in mind. She had written in the "So What?" column that it would be gross to drink out of a tin cup all the time. The only reason her family used tin cups when they went camping was because glass mugs might break when they were hiking.

"Hmmm." I gave her a puzzled look. "Why, then, do you suppose Salvador uses a tin cup all the time?"

"That's a good question," said Jo Anna. "A tin cup makes everything you drink taste like metal, especially if you leave something in it for very long."

"Jo Anna, I don't think rereading this again is going to help us answer this question. Could you think about your own life, and see if there would ever be a reason for someone to drink out of a tin cup all the time? Try to supply a possible, probable answer to your question."

Once again, a light went on. "Oh my gosh," she said. "Salvador drinks out of a tin cup all the time because he is so poor. Look," she continued. "Go back to the first part of the story. See how the author has described the house? They are totally poor."

I smiled again. "Jo Anna, you just did something a good reader does. You not only made a connection to your personal life to help you understand the text, but you also went back to the text for evidence to support your thinking."

"Wait," she said. "I'm not done. I have another connection. Last year there was this kid in my class like Salvador. He had messy hair and crooked teeth without braces. He wore the same clothes all the time and had really uncool shoes—you know the kind you buy at discount places? We made fun of him all the time. Do you think he looked the way he did because he was poor? That's so mean that we teased him. Maybe he couldn't help it. Maybe we should have cut him some slack."

This is why I became a high school English teacher. I love literature because it helps me understand people. It teaches me about the human soul. Corny, but nevertheless true. My job isn't about raising state test reading scores or getting kids to the advanced reading level on someone else's scale. My job is about teaching kids how to read and think about text in meaningful ways that help them better understand the people around them.

To a good reader, Jo Anna's inferences are obvious. I went back and tried to name Jo Anna's thinking for her. I pointed out that she made a personal connection and that the connection caused her to ask a question. Her question couldn't be answered by rereading, so she had to answer it by drawing a conclusion. She verified her conclusion by going back to the text to find evidence. She returned to her background knowledge and made another connection to a real person. Perhaps in time she will use literature to become a little more humane.

That evening I was thinking about Anthony and Jo Anna and wondering how we could re-create their thinking again and again with different pieces of text. A lot had happened that day, and I wanted to make some sense of it. I needed to identify for myself and my students what they had done that was so remarkable, and then build on it in my teaching and class activities over the next few days. I realized that the problem with the first sticky note activity was that I had stopped students' thinking too soon. I needed to get them to extend their thinking in other ways beyond the first reading (see Figure 2.4).

Strategy instruction is an ongoing process of adapting lessons and activities to the needs of students and the specific content you want them to tackle.

Figure 2.4 "So What?" Thinking Strategy

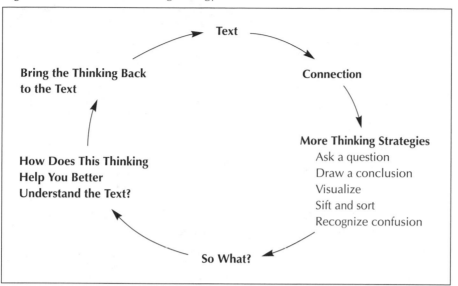

The following example demonstrates how Larry, a science teacher from my school, adapted the use of the double-entry diaries with the concept of "So What?" After I shared my "So What?" experience with him, Larry collected notes from double-entry diaries that students had used to hold their thinking while reading a chapter from his science textbook. He has taken examples from different students' notes and compiled them onto one sheet (see Figure 2.5). Larry then used this sheet as an overhead to review for the upcoming test.

What I do in the classroom is easy to replicate or adapt—there isn't a secret or magic formula. It can be used by any teacher, in any discipline.

I try to select interesting pieces of text that make kids want to know more about content. I model how I read—how I make sense of text and how I negotiate difficulty. I try to give students a reason to read by sharing with them possible purposes or how they can set a purpose that will help them remember what they read. I show students different ways to hold their thinking as they're reading so they can come back later and remember and reuse it. The following four principles guide most of my instruction:

Essential Elements of Comprehension Instruction

1. Assess the text students are expected to read. Is it interesting and pertinent to the instructional goal? Is it at the reading level of the students, or is it too difficult? If the text is too difficult, consider how you will make the text more accessible.

Figure 2.5 Science "So What?"

FACT	REASON FACTS ARE IMPORTANT
*Write the facts in your reading *Write about confusing ideas *Write unknown words	*Write your thinking about the facts.
A producer gets energy from the sun and uses it to produce food and oxygen.	The producer is the animal that is living to survive. It uses the suns energy and oxygen.
5.) Bacteria... are decomposers.	5. Does that mean that I'm being slowly eaten all the time?
3. niche - the job of an organism in the community.	3. The job of green plants is to produce food, oxygen, ect.
3. Producers also make oxygen during photosythesis.	3. So. algae makes oxygen? I thought only trees did that...
3. Animals that only eat plants are primary consumers.	3. This is very confusing because do primary consumers only have the job of eating plants?
4. Secondary consumers are animals that eat other animals.	4. This is very confusing because what could organisms that eat both plants and animals called
4. Decomposers	4. form their own group. living things that break down dead matter into simpler chemicals. very important.

2. Provide explicit modeling of your thinking processes. As an expert reader of your content, identify what you do to make sense of text. Share that information with your students.

3. Define a purpose and help students have a clear reason for their reading and writing. Make sure they know how the information they read and write will be used.

4. Teach students how to hold their thinking and give them opportunities to use the information they've held.

I think back to my days in high school and college as a student. I know I was taught a lot that I don't remember—or use. The information that I remember and use came from constructing meaning while learning about something new. My focus as a teacher has really shifted from covering a body of content and marching through a series of lessons to content comprehension. Strategy instruction is freeing, because I don't feel this incredible pressure to teach every classic novel or SAT vocabulary word or grammar rule.

Not Having Our Cake and Eating It Too

I know the biggest issue for any high school teacher thinking about making changes or additions to the curriculum is time. I hear this from almost every high school teacher I've met with over the last few years. What we're being asked to do is almost impossible. We're being asked to teach ridiculous amounts of material. We're being asked to teach kids how to read and write and think in sophisticated ways, and we're given a very, very short time in which to do it. Something has got to give.

An English teacher recently said to me, "I want my kids to read eight novels, but they're not doing it. What should I do?" I don't know if he was just expressing frustration or asking me for an easy solution, but I don't have one to give. My reply to teachers with these concerns and frustrations is this: I want to lose 30 pounds and eat chocolate cake all the time. It's not going to happen. I have to decide if I can eat chocolate cake once a month, or cut back in a different way to lose weight.

It's a trade-off. Only you can decide whether it is worth giving up some content for the time it takes to design comprehension instruction that means something to your students. If you don't value the thinking strategies, you won't give up content. If teaching kids to memorize what is in the textbook is most important to you, then this type of work won't be very successful.

We are also putting pressure on ourselves to cover vast amounts of content. Many state standards don't tell us that we have to teach certain novels in English classes. State standards don't always specify what years of U.S. history we have to cover in the history curriculum.

Many students will dutifully complete any strategy assignment from a teacher. After all, that's how I found myself one night facing a desk covered with sticky notes and banal comments. But that doesn't mean the assignment truly has any value for students, or is pushing them to think harder as readers.

I don't know if teachers can work any harder than they're already working, so we've got to find ways to make students carry more of the thinking load in our classrooms. As I walk out of school with my colleagues at the end of each day, we're all tired. We're carrying heavy bags of books and papers, and our shoulders are slumped. Meanwhile, our students bound past us to the parking lot, running and jumping down the steps two at a time, full of energy. I once heard someone say, "School should not be a place where young people go to watch old people work." We've got to figure out how to work smarter, because what we're being asked to do is really a challenge.

A young teacher from my district recently came to visit my classroom. He had told his teaching teammate he was coming in to see me teach. His teammate had read some of my work and said, "Take a lot of notes and find out what she does that's supposedly so great." This young teacher shared that request with me. He then smiled and said, "You're really not doing anything great. What you're doing is something I can take back and do in my classroom." Then he got a bit flustered and his face turned red, because he had said something that might be perceived as unkind.

I took his words as a compliment. What I'm doing is not unique or revolutionary. I use simple principles of good teaching to design comprehension lessons, activities, and materials. I give students models, time to practice, and time to think. It's common sense, and a lot of it comes from my own process as a reader.

What Works

1. Ask yourself, "Why am I doing this?" and "How will it help students think, read, or write more thoughtfully about my content?"

   Teaching Point: Good readers use reading, writing, and talk to deepen their understanding of content.

2. Remember that strategies are only options for thinking. One comprehension tool is not more important than another. There is no specific order, sequence, or template for introducing strategies to students.

   Teaching Point: Good readers have a variety of ways to think about text. They can make connections, ask questions, infer, and visualize, as well as sift and sort the value of different pieces of information.

3. Ask yourself as the expert of the content and the best reader in the class: "Is this activity authentic?" Would a mathematician, scientist, historian, or artist ever read in ways that approximate what you are asking of your students? If not, how could you make the activity more genuine?

   Teaching Point: Good readers don't need end-of-the-chapter questions or isolated skill sheets. They ask their own questions, based upon their need for a deeper understanding of specific aspects of the text.

4. Don't isolate strategy instruction into discrete, individual activities from day to day. Plan lessons based on student work from the previous day, using student response as a way to analyze how thoughtfully kids are approaching text.

Teaching Point: Good readers reread and return to text to build and extend their knowledge of specific concepts, or to enhance their enjoyment of texts they have enjoyed previously.

3

Parallel Experiences: Tapping the Mother Lode

If someone could teach these kids how to read, I could teach them science.
Melanie, high school science teacher

Not long ago I did a Saturday workshop with a group of high school teachers. I spent the day going over thinking strategies and helping them learn a little more about the comprehension process. The following Monday, I was to come back to the school and work with individual departments, helping teachers see how the work we did on Saturday would apply to their particular disciplines.

Monday went well until the last hour and a half, when I was to meet with the math and elective departments. It was obvious that these teachers weren't too pleased to have me there, since they were giving up their planning period. They were being told by administration in no uncertain terms that reading was now as important as content. Not only would they be teaching their kids to be better readers, but they would also have to figure out how to assess their students' reading and report back to their principal twice a month. The teachers were frustrated, but I also think they were scared. They were angry—not because they didn't want to cooperate, but because they didn't know how to do what was being asked of them.

I walked into the room and had barely put my presentation materials on a table before I was verbally accosted by a large man. He told me he couldn't teach his kids how to be better readers. "Sure you can," I said, trying to be reassuring.

"Oh yeah? Then you tell me how I'm supposed to teach reading when students don't have to read in my class."

"Don't read? What do you teach?" I asked.

"I teach industrial tech."

I wasn't even sure what "industrial tech" was. I asked him, "What do you do in industrial tech?"

Very slowly and loudly, he began, "We make things, like birdhouses and balsa-wood bridges. We have little contests to see who can build the strongest bridge with the least amount of wood and glue. We also build motors using schematas to inform our assembly. Do you know what a schemata is?"

"Well, no, I don't," I said.

"It's like a blueprint."

At this point, I realized that because this guy was so hostile, I probably couldn't teach him much. But, pragmatist that I am, I decided to get something out of the situation for myself.

My husband and I were in the midst of remodeling our kitchen. Because of this I know that not everyone can read a blueprint. It takes a certain skill that I don't possess. Just two days before, I had been trying to read the blueprint to find out where the kitchen window was going to go.

I wanted it to go over the sink, because 90 percent of my time in the kitchen is spent at the sink doing dishes. I found the window on the blueprint and proudly pointed it out to my husband. He took the blueprint from my hands, turned it around, and explained that I was pointing at the back door.

So I asked this teacher, "How do you read a blueprint?"

"What do you mean, how do I read a blueprint? I just read it."

"No, seriously, not everyone can read a blueprint. You're probably a pretty good reader of blueprints. Just tell me one thing you do when you read a blueprint."

I was really pushing this guy, not because I thought I was going to teach him anything about reading, but because I wanted to go back to my husband and redeem myself.

The guy must have sensed my commitment to the question, because he replied grudgingly, "Okay, I guess one thing that I do when I read blueprints or schematas or anything that has parts that have to fit together is look at the scale. If the parts don't match the scale, or the design doesn't fit the scale, the product won't come together."

Made sense. As a matter of fact a lot of people value this skill. Thinking back on my experience as a teacher of both elementary and high school kids, I remember many standardized tests that require students to be able to "read" a scale. Often these questions are not in the reading part of the test, but in the mathematics section. Sometimes scale reading is required in a geometry problem, or a distance problem where kids have to measure the distance from point A to point B. According to analyses I have seen, many students don't do well on these types of questions. But because these items are not a major part of the test, no one seems to throw a fit when students do poorly.

I filed this thought away, because now I was beginning to obsess about the birdhouses. How were the kids supposed to know how to build a birdhouse? I wouldn't know how to do it. Does this guy just take the wood and glue and nails, throw them on the floor, and tell the kids to "have at it"?

"So how do these kids know how to build the birdhouses?" I asked.

"Okay," he relented. "They do have to read directions."

Now, I'm not sure about kids everywhere, but I am sure about my own students. They are not very good at reading directions. As with blueprint reading, direction reading requires a certain skill.

Jaqueline Darvin, a reading specialist who worked with industrial technology teachers, marveled like me at how sophisticated this reading of blueprints and directions is, and how teachers who use these texts underestimate their reading skills:

> *Many of the vocational teachers claim that they don't like to read and are not good writers, yet I have been amazed by their skills in deciphering complex blueprints, instructional manuals, diagrams, and a variety of other difficult texts that relate to their trade areas. Working with these teachers and seeing what many of them can accomplish using highly technical texts has caused me to wonder why our society does not value the ways in which tradespeople use literacy in their lives. (Darvin 2000, p. 61)*

Just because we don't always value these skills in our society doesn't mean they aren't essential. And our students suffer because we don't think to teach these skills explicitly. Often students jump right into completing science projects or constructing responses to literature without reading the directions. They try to solve a math problem while ignoring charts and diagrams provided as part of the problem.

I couldn't help but think that if this industrial technology teacher could help the kids read directions and understand charts, he would not only help his students be more successful in his class, but might help other teachers of other disciplines. Likewise, if kids knew how to read and use scales, his students would be more successful when it came to designing and building.

If this teacher could teach his students how to read directions, I was pretty sure the English department could take care of teaching kids how to read poetry. I bet we could even get the science teachers to teach kids how to read data, charts, graphs, and tables. Social studies teachers could perhaps help students understand the value of being able to read with cause and effect in mind. And who better to help students learn how to read word problems than the math department?

The problem is that if language arts and English teachers are the only ones teaching reading, students aren't going to learn how to read different types of texts. Language arts and English teachers are just as burdened by an over-abundance of content as teachers in any other discipline.

Teachers of any subject are going to help their cause by teaching their students to be better readers of their content. The industrial technology teacher didn't need to teach kids how to read poetry. He needed to teach students how to read directions and blueprints and whatever else students read in his class. Perhaps he does this reading so automatically that he isn't even aware of the skills required for it.

The Importance of Mental Modeling

If teachers can begin to slow down their thinking and notice what they do as expert readers of their content, they will know how to design effective strategy instruction. They can show students through modeling their own reading process how proficient readers attack different kinds of texts.

It is important to give students models for ways of reading whenever we can. We see this a lot in athletics—coaches are great at this. They never tell a kid, "Just go hit a homer." They show them where to stand in the box and how to hold the bat and when to choke up.

I'm a pretty good reader of literature, but just because I can read and understand poetry doesn't mean I'm an expert math reader. Math teachers tell me all the time that they aren't very good readers. Some even say that is one of the reasons they became math teachers—because they didn't have to read very much. But math teachers are very good readers of math, better than any English teacher I've ever seen. They just have a different process for reading texts.

I suggest to frustrated teachers who worry that they don't know how to teach reading that they do know how to teach reading. They probably know how to read so well that they're not aware of all the thinking that they're doing to make sense of their content.

I've learned how to assist colleagues who teach reading, math, or technical texts by approaching any colleague who teaches in one of these areas. I give my colleague a piece of text, and say, "Hey, read this. Stop after the end of every paragraph and tell me what you're thinking." I write down what they say and look for patterns to find out what they're doing as good readers of that specific content.

For example, I've noticed when working with science teachers that they don't always start at the

Principles for Students Reading Math Textbooks
by Jim Donohue, Smoky Hill High School Math Teacher

- Speed kills. This is not a magazine.
- Read/reread with a pencil and paper in hand for notes.
- There are never enough commas. Insert your own pauses to help you slow down.
- Draw and label diagrams as you go.
- Think about related problems and procedures as you read.
- You can't just read; you have to "do it" as you go.
- Magic sometimes happens between the lines.
- Follow the instructions. ("Review the proof . . .")
- The figures and tables are *important*.
- The same number has different faces (one quarter, 1/4, .25)
- Mathematical writing has an idiosyncratic structure that when mastered will aid in constructing meaning.

beginning and read straight through to the end of science text. Many science teachers sometimes skip to the bottom of a science article and see if they recognize the author's or scientist's name. They'll check the reputation of the author, and they may look at the data or the graph. They may back up and read the abstract, and then start to read the article, or they may bounce around a little as they continue to read. That's different from an English teacher's approach to text. We usually start at the beginning and read methodically to the end.

I notice that math teachers read word problems differently than those who do not teach or read math. They usually read the entire problem all the way through, and then try to see how that problem relates to something in the real world. Then they look to see what information is given and what information is required. They see what their known variables are and what their unknown variables are. Nonmath readers don't really know how to do that kind of reading.

What I'm finding is we all have things in common as teachers, no matter what subject we teach. But I'm also finding that teachers of different contents read their texts differently. That's what we want to show our students.

> **Mental Modeling**
>
> Mental modeling does the following:
> - Gives students insights into how good readers and writers make sense of text.
> - Allows students to see options that are available to them. Students can see how good readers and writers decide what to do.
> - Helps students understand the complexities of reading and writing and that they are ongoing thinking processes.

Putting Ourselves on the Line

If teachers are going to make the process of reading visible, they can't sit safely at the edge. As older, more experienced readers, they have an obligation to talk aloud about groping for understanding or reaching for a genuine reading.

Dennie Palmer Wolf

Whenever I do a workshop for teachers, the first thing I do is give them a chance to read a challenging piece of text. My reasoning is that most teachers know their content so well and are so familiar with their reading material that they aren't aware of the thinking processes they use to make sense of text. By giving them something challenging to read, I can sometimes force teachers to see all that is involved in the meaning-making process.

One of my favorite texts to use is "Di Tri Berrese," a text I was given in a workshop years ago. I've never been able to find a source for it, but it is a wonderful short text for helping teachers see how they bring their previous histories and experiences as readers to texts.

Di Tri Berrese

Uans appona taim uas tri berrese: mamma berre, pappa berre, e bebi berre. Live inne contri nire foresta. NAISE AUS. (No mugheggia.) Uanne dei pappa, mamma, e beibi go tooda bice, onie, a furghette locche di doore.

Bai enne bai commese Goldilocchese. Sci garra nattinghe tu do batte maiche troble. Sci puscie olle fudde daon di maute; no live cromme. Den sci gos appesterrese enne slipse in olle beddse.

LEIEI SLOBBE!

Bei enne bai commese omme di tri berrese, olle sonnebronnde, enne send inne scius. Dei garra no fudde; dei garra no beddse. En ura dei goine due to Goldilocchese? Tro erre inne strit? Colle Puissemenne?

FETTE CIENZE!

Dei uas Italien Berrese, erne dei slippe onna florre.

Goldilocchese stei derre tri uicase; itte aute ausenomme, en guiste bicose dei eshe erre tu meiche di beddse, sci sei "Go to elle," enne runne omme criane to erre mamma, tellen erre uat sanificese di tri berrese uer.

Uatsiuse? Uara iu goine du—go comliene sittiolle?

I often have teachers work in small groups to make sense of "Di Tri Berrese." At first glance, the text appears to be written in Italian, or nonsense words. But as the teachers try to read it out loud, they begin to understand snippets of it. "Uans appona taim uas tri berrese" when read aloud sounds a lot like "Once upon a time was three bears."

But no one ever figures out that "no mugheggia" translates into "no mortgage." Many groups skip this phrase, and move on to passages they can understand more readily. After ten or fifteen minutes of working together, teachers see a range of strategies they've used to understand the text.

They note that phonetic pronounciation is just a small piece of the strategy puzzle. Merely sounding out the words won't help—they discover that they must also think hard as they read. They catch themselves making connections to the original story of the three bears. They find themselves asking questions about confusing parts, and substituting logical phrases for ones that make no sense.

They compare the dialect in the piece to what they've heard on *The Sopranos*, and read with those inflections in mind. To construct meaning for this short text, teachers must wrestle with the words and be flexible in their thinking, drawing on a wide range of background knowledge and experiences as readers. (A full "translation" of "Di Tri Berrese" is in the appendix, titled "The Three Bears.")

Using Text Features to Comprehend

I show the importance of exposing your struggles as a reader with unfamiliar text by modeling my own reading of difficult text for students and teachers. To know how to help readers get through difficult content, I must first identify what they are struggling with. Then I need to put myself in a similar situation and see how I as a good reader would negotiate the difficulty.

I was demonstrating this principle to some math teachers in my school who were trying to incorporate literacy instruction into the math curriculum. I wanted them to see that they could use their own textbooks, and that they didn't have to spend a lot of time coming up with reading lessons using other texts.

I borrowed the textbook from the integrated algebra class at our high school, a course designed to help kids who aren't math whizzes get through advanced algebra and geometry. I copied the page that the class had worked on the previous day, and made a transparency of it. I was unfamiliar with the content, and probably at the same level mathematically as the students. I wanted to model that certain features in textbooks are designed to make the reading easier. Figure 3.1 is a copy of the page.

For the demonstration, I worked with a class of ninth graders during their regular math period. Their math teacher and others from the department sat in the back of the room and observed. I began by "thinking aloud" (Davey 1983) as I read the first part of the textbook page on the overhead, writing notes in the margin as I talked in front of the students and my colleagues.

"I see that what's presented is a problem—one that I have no idea to how to solve." (See Note A on Figure 3.1.) I skimmed a bit more. Now I modeled patience. "I don't panic and quit. I keep on reading and trust that the book is going to show me how to solve the problem."

I focused on an example on the page that seemed to be designed to help a struggling mathematician like me. "Sure enough, in the sample response there is an example of how to get through the problem." (See Note B on Figure 3.1.) I studied the words and thought out loud about what they might mean.

I glanced at the back of the room and noticed that some of the math teachers were cringing. I continued on, knowing that I wasn't teaching students anything about math, but that perhaps I was teaching them something about reading a math text.

Finally, I came to a graphic on the left-hand side of the page. I told the students I thought this was an equation we needed to solve. (See Note C on Figure 3.1.) Dennis, the teacher of these students, could take it no longer. Fearing I would do irreparable math damage to his kids, he politely but forcefully corrected me. "That's not a formula, Cris. That's just a graphic—some artwork. It's found throughout the book."

"It is?" I asked.

"Yes, it doesn't mean anything."

Supo, a student in both the math class and my English class, came to my rescue. "Mr. Gournic, I thought that was a formula too, and that I just didn't get the math."

Figure 3.1 Algebra Text Excerpt

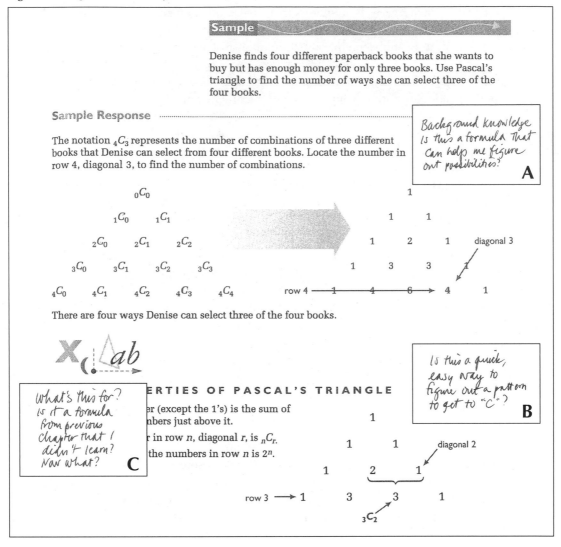

A few other kids muttered in agreement. Dennis and I looked at each other.

"It has to mean something," I said, "or the publisher wouldn't have put it in. Where else in the text is it found?"

"It's all over the place," Dennis replied. He began to flip through the book, demonstrating his point. But then he paused. "You know, I just realized something. Every time that graphic appears, a mathematical property is introduced. That's why it's in the book."

I didn't have the content knowledge in math to help the kids learn algebra and geometry the way Dennis did. He didn't believe the graphic was critical for understanding the content because he knows algebra. He didn't realize the graphic was an intentional part of the textbook design, put there to help readers organize their thinking. People like me don't automatically know these things. Many of the students didn't know it either. I guarantee they didn't know the graphic was a signal to the reader to look for a mathematical property.

As expert readers of our content, we take certain things for granted. Oftentimes we construct meaning without even being aware of doing so. We negotiate familiar text so automatically that we forget what it was like for us before we became expert readers. This is why I must identify something that my students are struggling with and then find a piece of text with similar content that isn't easy for me to read. It forces me to use all the strategies I take for granted when I read familiar text, and I can better tell what I am doing to make sense of the content.

Expert readers have different strategies for different content because the demands of different disciplines are so different.

> **Figuring Out the "How" of Modeling Our Reading**
>
> Depending upon the text, you might model how you do the following:
>
> * determine what is important
> * recognize and repair confusion
> * negotiate difficult reading situations
> * start new books
> * remember key words in previous chapters and use them in subsequent chapters
> * figure out unknown vocabulary
> * research topics
> * remember what you read
> * understand a poem
> * understand a word problem
> * infer meaning
> * recognize and use literary devices

Modeling How to Stay with a Text

One difficulty my students have is sticking with boring parts of text and not abandoning the reading altogether. When I am struggling to stick with a book, I first identify what causes me to want to abandon it. Lack of background knowledge, difficult vocabulary, and long descriptions all interfere with my comprehension. Knowing how the text is structured, as well as being able to read and paraphrase, helps me negotiate these difficulties.

I was preparing to do a lesson in a tenth-grade English classroom that was just beginning to read Mary Shelley's *Frankenstein*. It was a book that I "fake read" in college—I hadn't understood what I read back then, but had relied on Cliffs Notes and discussions with classmates to get the gist of the plot. Twenty years later, I didn't remember the book at all.

To do this lesson, I had to reread the book. I really struggled with the first part of it. It was so dull that my mind kept wandering from the text. Eventually I went to the Internet to find an overview of the novel, and I soon recalled that the story is told in "frames." The first part of the book is about a sea captain sailing to the Arctic. He sends letters to his sister in archaic language that seems to go on and on.

I managed to get past this first part of the story, only to find the second part almost as boring. In the second part of the book, the reader meets Dr. Frankenstein, who is picked up by the ship's captain. As the two become friends, Dr. Frankenstein begins to tell the story behind the creation and abandonment of the monster. All I kept thinking was blah blah blah—when are we going to get to the good part?

Finally, on page 53, Dr. Frankenstein starts to talk about procuring the body parts found in the slaughterhouses and graveyards:

> *I had returned to my old habits. I collected bones from charnet-houses and disturbed, with profane fingers, the tremendous secrets of the human frame. In a solitary chamber, or rather cell, at the top of the house, and separated from all other apartments by a gallery and staircase, I kept my workshop of filthy creation; my eyeballs were starting from their sockets in attending to the details of my employment. (Shelley 1963, p. 53)*

At last the book was getting exciting. Sadly, many of my students would have abandoned the book by page 53. They would have missed the gory parts, as well as the monster's evil deeds. What finally moved me was the last stretch of the book, when I experienced the sadness of the monster's isolation. Many students wouldn't get the same payoff I did from reading this novel because they would have quit, waiting for someone to tell them what they were supposed to have understood.

If I wanted the students to stay with this book, I would have to give them some support. I had had to do certain things for myself to get through the text. If I needed these strategies to keep reading, more than likely my students would need them too.

First, I needed an overall picture of the novel. I needed to know how the book was organized. Knowing that it was divided into three parts helped me remember that the good part was coming. If I stuck with it, I would at least learn the role of the ship's captain. It gave me a frame of reference, but more important, it helped me stick it out through the slow early section.

Second, knowing a bit about Mary Shelley and the time in which the novel was written helped me understand the book better. Knowing that Shelley intended it as a ghost story to meet a challenge somehow made it less intimidating. During a party one stormy night, Lord Byron challenged his guests to write the scariest story they could. Byron (being the genius that he was) picked the one written by Mary Shelley, the stepsister of his former lover. Armed with this knowledge, I was ready to teach the students.

Modeling *Frankenstein*

I entered the classroom, where students slouched in the perfectly arranged rows. The teacher introduced me: "This is Mrs. Tovani. She works with kids who don't read so well. I've invited her in to teach you to read better."

"I read just fine," came a murmur from the back row. "At least I read just fine when it comes to stuff that doesn't suck."

The teacher turned to me, signaling that it was my turn to start. "Hi," I began. No one responded. "You guys can call me Cris. And yes, I do work with struggling readers, but I also work with good readers. I understand that you are going to begin reading *Frankenstein*."

A collective groan permeated the room. "Yeah," I responded. "I know what you mean. It's probably not a book that you'd choose to read on your own. It's pretty hard too."

"That's for sure," said the same kid in the back who had just informed me he could read stuff that doesn't suck just fine.

"My job here today is to give you some strategies for getting through a tough book so that you understand it well enough to write an essay or pass a test."

I realized I would be in this classroom only one day. I couldn't give them all they needed to know in forty-nine minutes. I quickly gave them some background knowledge on Mary Shelley, then moved to the overall structure of the novel. I reassured them that although the piece had some difficult vocabulary at first, they didn't need to know every word they read.

I talked as I passed out copies of pages 53 and 54 of the novel. I had decided that these pages were the most likely to pique their interest. The only way I know how to do this is to let them read a good part. I would model questioning, a strategy that often helps me think about difficult pieces of text.

I began to read the passage out loud, but I didn't get very far. I read a paragraph and then stopped to model my thinking. "What is this guy doing? Is he in a morgue?"

I modeled a few more questions before a girl in the front stopped me and said, "Don't you know?"

"Don't I know what?"

"The answers to your questions?"

She'd caught me. "Well, I know now because I've read the book a couple of times. But I didn't know the answers to these questions the first time I read it."

It's important for students to know that you are the expert in the room, but it is also important that you model what it was like for you as a first-time reader of the piece. It's equally important for you to help them see how your thinking changes as you become more familiar with the text. I knew this girl could shut me down in an instant, causing me to lose credibility with the students, if she thought I wasn't being honest.

So I rephrased the question into a comment. "The first time I read this book, I was wondering where Dr. Frankenstein was. I didn't know if he was in a graveyard or a morgue. It didn't occur to me that he was in a slaughterhouse."

"He was in a slaughterhouse? You mean he was looking for animal parts too?" asked a tall boy in the back.

"Great question. I'm not sure," I admitted. "Let's write it down so we don't forget it." I jotted it down on the chart tablet attached to the chalkboard.

"But now, I wonder if Stephen King got some of his ideas from Mary Shelley, because this sounds like a book he could have written."

I looked up at the girl who had called me on the carpet about the honesty of my questions. She nodded. "Good question."

I read on, but only briefly. The same girl raised her hand. "Why is this guy collecting body parts?"

I recorded her question on the chart paper. "That's a great question." I stopped writing to point out that this girl had just done something good readers do. She was asking questions to which she didn't know the answers.

Instantly another hand shot up. "What's a charnet house?" I recorded the question without supplying an answer.

"Is this guy's laboratory in his house? Is he a psycho?"

I continued to record questions. It's helpful if questions are written down so they can be returned to later. Authentic questions can drive the reading and guide the learning well after the lesson is finished.

After several minutes of reading and noting questions, I gave the students an opportunity to read the rest of the two pages on their own. I encouraged them to write their questions in the margins. While they were reading, I circulated, reading the questions they had written. Many were quite good.

I found a student in the back who wasn't marking text. I asked him to point out where he was in the passage. He showed me that he was on the first paragraph. I feigned farsightedness and asked him to read that part to me because I couldn't see it without my glasses. He began, but struggled to decode. It was obvious that this book was too difficult for him. I took over for him and read. I told him I would be his reader and secretary. I would write down his questions, but he would have to supply them.

I read, he asked questions, I wrote. We got through the first page, and I paired him with the boy sitting next to him. They shared the task. I returned to the front of the room as I saw that the bell was about to ring.

"Before the bell rings," I said, "let's add some of your questions to the chart." The room erupted with questions, and I wrote as quickly as I could. The last question asked was one I didn't write down. It came from the boy in the back who struggles only with "reading that sucks." He asked, "Can we read this whole book?"

I knew how to get students interested in *Frankenstein*, because I knew my content as an English teacher and my process as a reader. Any teacher is the best reader of the content they are teaching. If you're able to slow your thinking down a little and notice things that you do when you read content material, you can teach the strategies you use to students. You will then have the beginnings of your specific reading curriculum for students in your discipline.

What Works

1. Identify what students are struggling with. It may be any of the following:
   - rereading text for a second time
   - reading difficult or uninteresting text
   - starting a book
   - making sense of graphs
   - understanding how to read a word problem
   - making sense of poetry

   Teaching Point: Good readers have a variety of strategies they know how to use flexibly, depending on the task at hand. Teacher modeling can help students learn to identify what strategies are best suited to the needs of the specific text they will be tackling.

2. Select a challenging piece of text to model reading for students that will allow you to experience the same difficulty they will face.
   - Use a piece that is unfamiliar and challenging.
   - Target thinking at how to handle the struggle.
   - Notice what you do as a good reader of that material to overcome the struggle.

   Teaching Point: Good readers are aware of their thinking. They know what they are doing when their reading goes well. When understanding breaks down, they can consciously apply strategies to reconstruct meaning.

3. Share with students how you overcame the struggle. What did you do as an expert reader of the content to get through the text?
   - How does rereading the text benefit your thinking?
   - How do you stay engaged in an uninteresting, difficult piece?
   - How do you start and stay with a book?
   - Do you notice titles when reading graphs, word problems, or poems?

   Teaching Point: Good readers automatically apply new strategies to aid comprehension when they begin to struggle with text. Teachers can help readers develop their strategies if they are not yet automatic for students.

4

Real Rigor: Connecting Students with Accessible Text

If the reading is too hard, I just get the Cliffs Notes or skim through chapters. If I can't get the Cliffs Notes, I just listen to what the teacher and kids in the class say.
Jay, high school sophomore

Several years ago I was given the daunting task of figuring out why so many ninth graders in our high school were flunking U.S. history. At the time, freshmen were flunking U.S. history more often than any other class. As I began to investigate, two problems became obvious. There was too much content to cover (and not enough time to cover it), and the textbook used for the class was too difficult.

I realized I needed the help of the social studies department chairman to solve this problem. I told him that the textbook the kids were using was inaccessible. With a deadpan look on his face he responded, "So what you are saying is that the text is too hard?"

"Yes," I replied. "I think it is too hard, too long, and too boring."

"And you're suggesting that we replace it?"

"Well, yes, that would be terrific." I was thinking to myself, This is a lot easier than I thought it was going to be.

"Forget it," he snapped. "We just spent thirty thousand dollars replacing those textbooks. We're going to be using them for the next ten years. And if you're suggesting we take away the textbooks, you can forget that too. Our youngest and most inexperienced teachers are the ones teaching U.S. history. They need that textbook. What are they supposed to use without it?"

Obviously the textbooks were going to be the students' primary source of information for quite some time. Richard Strong (Strong et al. 2002) does not foresee textbooks becoming obsolete any time soon.

Like it or not, textbooks are here to stay. Even as technology changes the nature of nonfiction reading into a multisensory, multitext experience, the textbook—that single, hardbound, seemingly complete container of a year's worth of content—remains a constant. . . . Even if we choose to reject textbooks completely—cast them aside as biased, poorly written, or demotivating—it turns out that we would be doing our students a disservice in preparing them for college, where the first-year student is asked to read, on average, eighty pages per class per week, with most of the load coming from textbooks. (p. 2)

In my head I calculated what year it would be when we could order new U.S. history textbooks. The department chairman's concerns were valid. I had to come up with an alternative that would support teachers and give kids something interesting and readable, keeping in mind two real concerns of all content teachers: too much content and not enough accessible text.

The curriculum in U.S. history classes increases by 365 days every year. I realize that purists don't consider something history until it is at least twenty-five to thirty years old. However, the commonsense side of me says that any good history teacher works hard to connect current events of the day with historical events to help students make sense of the past.

The only way U.S. history teachers can cover course content that begins with Native Americans and progresses to modern day is if they lecture and feed the information to the students. There is no time to allow students to read unless the reading is done at home. We all know how successful that is, especially for struggling readers.

Teachers end up lecturing so they can deliver the maximum amount of content. The problem with this is that the teachers end up doing most of the work. Students aren't getting an opportunity to construct meaning. They might remember the information for a multiple-choice test, but then they usually forget it. Teachers are frustrated because students don't remember information from previous chapters, so they constantly feel as though they have to back up and reteach material.

Some students are seeing textbooks for the first time when they enter ninth grade. When students have to read their textbooks, they usually aren't very good at it, because they haven't had much practice with these difficult texts. Richard Allington (2002b) addresses the problem of harder books in the following passage:

Unfortunately, the idea of harder textbooks has captured the attention of educators and policymakers interested in raising academic achievement. But harder books won't foster the growth of content learning. Think about your own attempts to acquire new content knowledge. Imagine you want to learn about building a website. Do you reject the books you might use because they are too

easy? Do you say to yourself, "Gosh, only 11 words on this page that I can't pro-
nounce—not hard enough for me!" (p. 39)

U.S. history can be fascinating. But when teachers are faced with classes of
more than thirty students of widely varying reading abilities, choices are limited.
The course textbook seems like the best solution, but only if students are actually
reading it. The reading material is often above their grade level and inconsider-
ately written. Concepts are introduced too quickly. Too many vocabulary words
are thrown at students, with not enough opportunity to use them. Students'
background knowledge on the topic may be limited, so they having nothing to
connect the new reading to.

The pressure to emphasize "coverage" over content is what got us in trouble
in the first place. Janet Allen (2000) says it this way: "I think this is one of the
things that has left most of us with such sketchy understandings of historical
events: someone tried to cover all the events rather than help us understand the
social and political concepts several events might have shared" (p. 129).

If students are to understand what they read, then teachers must find text
that they can read to supplement the textbook—as well as give them time to
practice new strategies for understanding the reading during class.

What Is Accessible Text and Where Do I Find It?

Accessible text has become the cornerstone of my instruction. When I use text
that is interesting, well written, and appropriately matched to the level of my students, my life as a teacher gets easier. Accessible text can come in a variety of
forms. It is not "low level" or "dumbed down." Most of the time it is of high
interest, but often it is found in contexts outside of school. It doesn't have a con-
trolled vocabulary, and it usually doesn't come out of a textbook. Accessible text
is pleasant to the eye and interesting to read. I usually find accessible text in
places that cater to people who really read.

A lot of my accessible text comes from newspapers and magazines. It is
timely, well written, and short. Often it can be read in one sitting or in a class
period. Accessible text helps students make a connection between school sub-
jects and the real world because it helps them experience reading that is done in
the real world.

Accessible Text Doesn't Sacrifice Rigor

"The only place where you and I disagree is that I want more rigor in my classroom than you do."

For a second I was taken aback. Rick, a young and energetic English teacher, threw out this comment at the end of an hour-long discussion about current reading and writing practices. We were discussing instructional changes that we wanted to see over the next four years in our department when Rick tossed out his insinuation that I didn't value rigor.

I drove home, thinking about how I should respond, when it dawned on me: some teachers might be confusing rigor with unrealistic expectations. Is it rigor to assign a tough textbook chapter when no one in the class can understand it? Is it realistic to think that just because you are teaching a tenth-grade class all readers are reading at the tenth-grade level? By the way, what exactly is the "tenth-grade level"? Could it be that when I ask teachers to find text students can read and understand, some interpret it as lowering instructional expectations?

I have no intention of lowering standards of rigor, regardless of students' ability level. My intention is to give students something to read that is worthy of their time, something that they actually have the potential to understand—and maybe even finding a piece of text that will turn kids on to the content.

What one student considers rigorous reading might spell defeat to another. For example, Rick would consider running a mile a mere warm-up. His rigorous workout may include a five-mile run and forty-five minutes of lifting weights. His workout would be very different from mine. I could barely ride a bike five miles, let alone run that distance. If I use the same training regimen as Rick, I will be defeated the first day I attempt it. However, if I train and spend time working up to five miles, I can eventually achieve that level of fitness.

There may be other factors that I might not be able to change. For example, my age is a disadvantage, as is my asthma and my lack of desire to run. These factors must be taken into account if I am going to be held to the same standard of rigor. Chances are no matter how hard I work out, I will never be able to reach the same level of fitness as Rick when it comes to running. If I am constantly held to his level, I will give up and quit running altogether.

How does this translate to the classroom? If we are constantly giving students text that is too hard for them to read, they may get through it, but probably not without cheating. Many of my students who are struggling readers feel defeated before they even begin. Just because students are tenth graders doesn't mean they are all capable of reading a geometry textbook. I must consider how much reading they have done in the past, and how well they read now.

I also need to remember what it feels like to read something for the first time. I can't expect my students to be able to read and understand for the first time text that I work at over a period of time to understand. I don't just "get" a piece of text the first time I read it. I have to work hard to understand it so I can use it in my instruction. It isn't fair for me to spend days or even years planning instruction around a text, and expect my students to read and understand the concepts the first time through—especially knowing that reading comprehension drops when readers are reading unfamiliar information. I want to challenge students to think, in the way Hyde and Bizar (1989) write about:

> *We have found that students care more when they are encouraged to think, when they are challenged to an intellectual wrestling match. We don't mean challenged by ideas that are so abstract that students are not intellectually ready for them; that kind of challenge invites frustration. We mean challenging them to understand through contexts that are meaningful, where ideas come with examples and explanations, where the intellectual processes are not simple and obvious, where answers cannot readily be memorized. All these processes should occur within a classroom climate that encourages perseverance, allows time to think and work things out, and does not quickly judge and penalize mistakes. (p. 14)*

For Helen, who is reading at about the fourth-grade level, a science essay out of *Kids Discover* magazine is a rigorous read. For her to read and understand the tenth-grade biology book is impossible. When left to her own devices, she will either cheat to get the assignment done or give up. However, with support from the teacher, background knowledge about the piece, and lots of practice reading text that she can manage on her own, she might build her fluency enough to someday read more difficult science text. When students are always given text that is too hard for them to read on their own, they begin to associate school reading with reading that is pointless.

I also think of Tiesha, a ninth grader who came to my high school in the third quarter without a single credit. She was a struggling reader. My initial assessment was that her reading was comparable to the average third or fourth grader.

One day during reading workshop, I watched Tiesha as she plowed through *To Kill a Mockingbird*. I was fascinated that she never lifted her head for the full forty minutes. Perhaps she reads better than I think, I mused as I headed to her desk. I could tell she was almost finished with the book, and I was curious to see how she liked it. I pulled my chair next to her and said, "So, what part are you on?"

I was guessing that she was at the exciting part where Boo Radley emerges from his home to save Jem from being killed.

Tiesha looked up from her book and said, "I'm at the end."

"I can see that, Tiesha. What I mean is, what is happening right now in the book?"

"I'm not sure. I don't really get it," she admitted.

"What's the last part that you remember?" I prodded.

"I don't really remember any of it." With big brown eyes, she looked at me and said, "I don't know what's happening, and the worst part of all is that I have to answer all these questions."

I asked her to read a little bit out loud for me. It was clear that she couldn't understand what she was reading because she could barely decode the words. Tiesha is rare. Many students won't sit for forty minutes trying to read text that is too difficult for them. More often they become behavior problems and start to disturb others.

I explained to Tiesha's English teacher that she was a struggling reader and that *To Kill a Mockingbird* was probably too difficult for her to get through on her own. He asked me what I wanted him to do about it. I asked if there was an alternative assignment that she could read and told him I would be happy to help her when she was in reading workshop class with me. He said that if he gave Tiesha an alternative assignment, he would have to give the entire class an alternative assignment.

I'm not sure I understand his logic. It is definitely more work for the teachers, but if we don't find text that kids such as Tiesha can read, they will never improve as readers.

The next day, I took Tiesha into my office and showed her a Web site that has all kinds of readable information about *To Kill a Mockingbird.* No, it wasn't the same as reading the novel, but she had already done that and gotten nothing out of it. Perhaps alternative text would help her construct some meaning around the book, and perhaps several years from now Tiesha will take another stab at reading it.

If we don't begin to find accessible text for all adolescent readers, they will continue to fail, only to become someone else's problem the following year. More students will become turned off to the content we love.

I shared Tiesha's story with Rick. He thought for a moment and said, "Do you think we focus too much on teaching our curriculum, and don't devote enough time to teaching our students?" I think Rick is right. When we don't know our students as readers, we have unrealistic expectations for rigor. We've got to figure out how well they can read and base the reading on that.

Alternative Texts

I know this is easier said than done, but teachers have to begin somewhere to find materials students can read in addition to textbooks. With the seed in place, Rick began looking for ways to give alternative assignments to struggling readers. He decided that if kids weren't reading, they weren't going to get better at reading.

Together Rick and I began searching for "companion pieces." For example, the book *Finn* (2001) by Matthew Olshan can be read by less able readers in place of *Huckleberry Finn*. *Finn* is about a young girl who is being raised by her grandparents because her dad has died and her mom is abusive. The girl, Finn, fakes her death and sets off to free her grandparents' pregnant Mexican maid, who has immigrated to the United States illegally. She is trying to get to California to find the father of the baby before the baby is born, and some of the plot points and themes roughly parallel those in *Huckleberry Finn*.

Finn doesn't have the same literary genius as Mark Twain's *Huckleberry Finn*, but it does give students something that's a bit easier to read, as well as a way to explore similar themes.

Text Sets: A Supplemental Alternative

Another alternative for finding accessible text for kids, especially to support concepts in textbooks, is an idea called text sets. I'm sure I stole this idea from elementary teachers. In elementary classrooms around the country you find libraries organized by authors, genres, or themes. Upon entering one of these classrooms, an observer might see books organized in brightly colored containers with neatly labeled signs. The signs are often genre-specific or author-specific. For example, the box labeled "Nature Poems" would hold books containing poems about nature. An author container might have different books written by Lois Lowry. This is a great way to begin helping kids recognize genre traits and authors' styles.

I liked this idea and wondered why middle and high school teachers couldn't use the same notion and adapt it a little. Instead of genre, for example, containers can be organized by units of study. Author text sets would still be appropriate. Classes such as science and math could have text sets about famous scientists and mathematicians. History classrooms could categorize text sets around famous explorers or politicians. Writing in *Educational Leadership*, Gail Ivey (2002) urges teachers to make additional sources available to students:

> *When teachers make the transition from textbook only classrooms to multitext classrooms, the focus of study becomes concepts rather than the content of one particular book. Students gain both a broad perspective and an in-depth sense of the subject matter from reading many texts on the*

Text Sets

- contain a wide variety of written texts;
- contain materials that vary in length, difficulty, and text structure;
- contain examples of text that are relevant, interesting, and accessible to most students;
- give students several options for obtaining information;
- provide opportunities for students to practice reading strategies and learn content information.

same topic. I know of no one textbook that contains enough information to help a student become even mildly expert on any topic. (p. 21)

There are many ways to adapt text sets to different content areas to provide accessible text that focuses on the information or concepts to be learned.

Many struggling readers in U.S. history are also in my reading workshop class, so I decided to experiment with U.S. history text sets first. My plan was to create text sets around major topics of study. These topics of study also aligned with the current U.S. history curriculum.

I purchased ten purple containers with lids and handles and set about selecting major topics of study, using the U.S. history textbook as my guide. I reasoned that if students could read about U.S. history in my class, they would build background knowledge that would help them in history. They might also improve their reading ability because the text was accessible.

What Goes in a Text Set?

The secret of creating a text set is to have several texts about a topic that vary in length, format, and genre.

Examples of U.S. history text sets that my students and I have built include the following:

American Indians
Revolutionary War
Civil War
Slavery
World War II
Vietnam War
Transportation through time
Civil rights
Musicians
Athletes

For example, the World War II text set contains these materials:

Rosie the Riveter by Penny Colman. New York: Crown Publishers, 1995.
    This is a nonfiction book with many photos.
I Had Seen Castles by Cynthia Rylant. Orlando, FL: Harcourt Brace, 1993.
    This novel is a love story set during the war.
Hiroshima by John Hersey. New York: Vintage, 1946, 1985. This is a nonfiction collection of interviews done after the bombing of Hiroshima, with

follow-up interviews almost four decades later in the second editions.

I Never Saw Another Butterfly: Children's Drawings and Poems from Terez Concentration Camp, 1942–44, edited by Hana Volavkova. New York: Schocken Books, 1993. Foreword by Chaim Potok. This is a poignant collection of poems and illustrations by children.

Smithsonian magazine, March 1994. With a cover photo of Rosie the Riveter, this issue is dedicated to women's contributions during World War II.

Kids Discover World War II, vol. 10, June 2000. A great magazine loaded with information about World War II, this issue has lots of white space, without insulting older readers.

Copy of original letter "Regulations for Prisoners," USS *Sanctuary* Ah-17, August 5, 1945, Wm. Van C. Brandt, commanding officer. This letter was given to me by a colleague whose father was a prisoner of war in World War II.

"Totally Devoted," *Daily Times-Call,* June 17, 2002. In this article from the Longmont, Colorado, newspaper, a couple celebrate their seventieth anniversary and recount the personal sacrifices people have to make during wartime.

Examples of Accessible Text
Poems
Short nonfiction selections
Fiction
Picture books
Newspaper articles
Short stories
Vignettes
Biographical information
Internet pieces
Student writing
Mathematical writing
Lists
Historical recounts
Photos
Postcards
Primary sources
Quotes
Song lyrics
Stamps
Letters and journals
Pictures of artwork
Calendars
Recipes
Brochures
Maps
Charts and graphs
Catalogs
Menus
Almanacs
Magazine articles

Japanese flier (in original language with translation) propaganda about the "Gumbatsu" (enemy) air raids, and other photos from fliers depicting U.S. invasion. Students love to see the actual documents used.

"Unhappy Endings" by Ann Banks, *Woman's Day,* October 7, 1997. In this essay a parent complains about the use of *Faithful Elephants: A True Story of Animals, People, and War,* a children's picture book used in her daughter's classroom. She says she doesn't want her daughter exposed to negative depictions of war. This makes a nice companion piece to the picture book *Faithful Elephants* by Yukio Tsuchiya.

Household ledger of expenses (handwritten), 1942. This account book kept by my grandma Lowe illustrates the effect of the war from an economic standpoint.

My Hiroshima by Junko Morimoto. Sydney: Collins, 1987. The Japanese perspective on Hiroshima is presented in this children's book, building background knowledge.

"Trail Breakers" by James Daugherty. In Lee Bennett Hopkins, ed., *Hand in Hand.* New York: Simon and Schuster, 1994. U.S. westward expansion is compared with the Atomic Age in this poem—a quick way to help students see the progression of technology.

Faithful Elephants: A True Story of Animals, People, and War by Yukio Tsuchiya. Boston: Houghton Mifflin, 1997. This short picture book creates curiosity in students and shows how the innocent are ravaged by war.

Words of Inspiration crossword puzzle cut out from the newspaper with clues linked to World War II events.

Original World War II recruitment postcards used by the U.S. government. These authentic pictures help readers visualize something from the era.

I also developed a guide sheet, which is in the appendix, to help students work their way through the text set, and make connections between the readings and their work in history.

Science teacher Amy Krza and English teacher Ann Meisel, both of Smoky Hill High School, decided to work together to develop a text set of short science-related writing to help students learn how science writing differs from fiction. Ann selected a diverse range of texts, both fiction and nonfiction. She was looking for short, vivid descriptions of natural phenomena that could provoke a more emotional response in students than typical science writing. The collection included excerpts from the following:

Cannery Row, a novel by John Steinbeck, has a short passage with a fascinating description of an octopus.

The Bean Trees, a novel by Barbara Kingsolver, was selected for her description of "the life cycle of wisteria."

Pilgrim at Tinker Creek, Pulitzer Prize–winning nonfiction by Annie Dillard, has many good passages for the text set, including descriptions of a giant water bug, a praying mantis, a Polyphemus moth, and pine processionaries.

The Medusa and the Snail: More Notes of a Biology Watcher by Lewis Thomas is a collection of short essays. A couple in the text set are "Mars" and "On Warts."

"Africa's Wild Dogs," by Richard Conniff, in *National Geographic.*

"Under Water," by Anne Fadiman, in *The New Yorker.*

"LuLu, Queen of the Camels," by Cullen Murphy, in *The Atlantic Monthly.*

I am working on new text sets to support readers in ninth- and tenth-grade English classes. Below is a list of sets that will align with our building's ninth-grade literature curriculum.

Shakespeare

As a department, we have agreed that students at each grade level will read something from William Shakespeare. This will be an author text set containing biographical information about Shakespeare, as well as picture-book versions of his dramas. There are also examples of cartoons and advertisements that refer to Shakespeare and his work.

Famous quotes as well as lesser-known facts about Shakespeare are housed in this text set. There are actual pieces written by Shakespeare as well as annotated versions of his writing, and magazine articles and historical information about his life and times.

The Greeks

Most ninth graders in our building read *The Odyssey,* and many students struggle with its language. The numerous references to Greek gods, monsters, and heroes also make it a difficult read. This text set contains more readable versions of *The Odyssey,* including picture books, as well as books that have information about Greek gods, monsters, and heroes. Information about the literary structure of the epic poem, maps of Ancient Greece, and related articles from nonfiction sources such as magazines and newspapers round out this set.

To Kill a Mockingbird

This text set is designed to be organized around a classic piece of literature. *To Kill a Mockingbird* is a great book, but it is often wasted on the young. To help students appreciate its richness, there are several selections in this text set about the time period and setting. Interesting tidbits about the author, Harper Lee, are also included, as well as pictures and information about Jim Crow laws and the civil rights movement.

These text sets will grow and change throughout the year. New ones will be added next year as current ones are replaced because of changing curriculum requirements. These text sets can be used by students to build background knowledge and fluency, as well as other literacy skills.

Here are examples of text sets that could be developed for other content areas:

Evaluation of Text Sets

Text sets are *not* designed to catch kids who aren't reading. Text sets are designed to give reluctant readers a choice of interesting and accessible text. They provide opportunities for learning and practicing reading strategies.

The use of text sets can be evaluated in the following ways:

Writing letters to future users of the sets to include with the materials.

Observing students as they use the sets and conferring with them.

Asking students to compare and contrast pieces in a text set.

Recording questions to ponder and research. (These questions can also be attached to the lid of the box for others to see.)

Marking interesting and important places in the text with sticky notes that describe connections made by the reader.

Figure 4.1 Criteria for Selecting Science Reading for Text Sets

In "Using Various Genres to Promote Science Practices," Margaretha Ebbers develops these categories and criteria for selecting books for text sets in science:

Nonfiction Genre	Use	Find Books That
Reference	Account of phenomena	Limit assertions Contain phrases such as "scientists think" or "this suggests"
Explanation	Explain causality Describe purpose	Limit assertions Demonstrate tentativeness Show how/why the explanation was generated
Field Guides	Organize and classify	Clearly show relationships
How-To	Illustrate specific procedures	Contain experiments within contexts Demonstrate variety of procedures
Narrative Expository	Information through narrative mode	Tell a story first Embody what is known in the scientific community
Biography	Develop the community of scientists	Show male and female scientists Include non-Western scientists
Journal	Illustrate practices	Portray both male and female scientists Show many dimensions of their lives

Language Arts *80 (September 2002): 40–50.*

Health Class: Text sets could be designed around tobacco and alcohol use, illegal drugs and at-risk behaviors, exercise, diet, and the World Wrestling Federation. *Possible Uses:* When students can't participate in class for any reason, they could read a text set for the period and complete a double-entry diary instead of sitting on the bleachers watching their grade drop and their waistline expand. At least they'd be getting smarter.

Science Class: Text sets could be designed around current units of study, using Margaretha Ebbers's criteria for selecting text (see Figure 4.1). Current news articles and various genres exploring the topics of cloning, genetic engineering, or environmental pollution that connect science to the real world could be included. *Possible Uses:* When students do poorly on a test, they could read a text set and write a paragraph to practice summarizing.

Math Class: Text sets could be designed around famous mathematicians, numbers found in nature, patterns, interesting number combinations, or graphs of useful information.

When I taught in an elementary school years ago, we used to talk a lot about "just-right books"—finding a book that wasn't too easy, but wasn't too hard for each student. I think that as kids move on to middle and high school, the material they're asked to read is too hard. If kids are always reading textbooks that are too hard for them, their reading is never going to improve. If we want to ensure that our students' reading ability grows, we have to give them text that they can practice with, at a level of difficulty that is appropriate. It's an ongoing challenge that never gets easier, but it's one we need to face.

What Works

1. Provide a choice of reading materials. Don't limit students' ability to think about your content because the textbook is too hard. Collect accessible text related to your field.

   Teaching Point: Good readers know that background knowledge improves comprehension. If they have limited knowledge about a topic, they find resources to build their background knowledge. This enables them to read more difficult text.

2. Demonstrate how your content connects to the real world. Current events— whether local or international—can almost always be applied to concepts being taught in the classroom.

   Teaching Point: Good readers use information from a variety of sources to connect to daily events that affect their lives. They blur boundaries between information sources and look for patterns.

3. Give students opportunities to read provocative text. If it is boring to you, it will be boring to them.

   Teaching Point: Good readers know when to abandon a text. They will not read text that has no information or use in their daily lives.

4. Don't expect the textbook to do your job. You are the expert on the content. Use the reading material, including the textbook, to go beyond the learning in the classroom.

   Teaching Point: Good readers apprentice themselves to content experts. They rely on those who have mastered the content to demonstrate through reading, writing, and talking how learning happens in a discipline.

5

"Why Am I Reading This?"

I am not a speed reader. I am a speed understander.

Isaac Asimov

Lisa, a varsity cheerleader and honors student, asks to speak to me privately after class about two months into the semester. She is concerned about what we were doing in her college-prep English class. She informs me that she isn't taking the class because she needs the credit. As a matter of fact, she already has more than enough credits to graduate. She has her own reasons for taking CP English, and they have nothing to do with fulfilling graduation requirements. Lisa has heard through the grapevine that this class will help her prepare for college—that it will make her a better reader.

"So, Lisa, what's the problem?" I ask.

"The problem," Lisa scoffs, "is my reading. Not only is my reading not getting better, but it's getting worse."

"Worse?" I ask. "How could your reading be getting worse?"

Lisa tilts her head to the side, flicks back her hair, and says, "Oh, I think you know the answer to that."

I assure her that I don't know the answer, and I encourage her to enlighten me. What she says next stuns me.

"Everything that you are asking us to do in here is slowing me down. My reading is not getting faster—it's getting slower."

"Why do you think you are slowing down?" I ask.

"I have to slow down because everything you are asking us to do requires me to think."

It dawns on me that Lisa is equating fast reading with good reading. She doesn't see reading as thinking. She views it as a race. Lisa doesn't understand that good readers adjust their pace as when they read.

To read well, one has to have a more significant purpose than reading to finish first. Janet Allen (2002) says we too often fail to show students how to set a purpose: "For many students, . . . purpose setting [has] been overlooked as part of the modeled instruction and guided practice that are critical to strategic reading" (p. 57).

The purpose readers set for themselves as they read affects comprehension in several ways. First, it determines the speed of the reading. If readers are scanning the phone book for a name, they can read very quickly. If they are reading a math word problem, they most likely read slowly to catch important information. Purpose also determines what the reader remembers. When readers have a purpose, they tend to remember more of the text.

Recognizing that purpose often determines what is important and what a reader remembers has major implications for content instruction. It means that teachers have to be clear in their reasons for assigning the reading. Students need to know what those reasons are so they can better determine what is important. Although we know why reading is important, many students do not, according to high school teacher Kelly Gallagher (2003):

> For people who like to read, searching for reading reasons at first seems silly. We adults have already found a multitude of reasons to read. Sometimes we are conscious of these reasons; but often, I suspect, many of these reasons have become internalized. We often take them for granted because we have long ago acknowledged their value. We motivate ourselves to read, consciously or unconsciously, because the benefits of doing so are ingrained in us. Unfortunately, this is not often the case with our students. Just because we have internalized a number of reasons why reading enriches our lives doesn't mean we should assume our students have done the same. (p. 139)

There are many ways to help students begin to link reading and purpose. One Monday morning, I asked the seniors in my CP English class to jot down on a slip of paper an example of reading they had done over the weekend. I then asked them to note the purpose of the reading on the same sheet of paper. A quick look at some of the student responses showed a range of reading skills and purposes used naturally in their daily lives (see Figure 5.1). The challenge for me becomes helping these students become aware of the different purposes of school reading tasks.

Defining Purposes Before Teaching

Sometimes our problem as adult readers is that we see too many reasons or purposes for our students to read a text. Several years ago, I began working with

Figure 5.1 Student Weekend Reading Purposes

Luke

This weekend I read a little *Harry Potter* with the sole purpose to make good clear pictures in my head so I could try to really enjoy myself.

Christina

This weekend I read *Soap Opera Digest,* mostly the parts on *General Hospital.* My purpose for reading it was to find out the new cast for *General Hospital* and to see if there was an article on my favorite character, Vanessa Marcil (Brenda).

Jay

This weekend I read the movie listings online. My purpose was to find a movie to watch at a certain time.

Lindsay

This weekend I read my bank statement. My purpose for reading this was to find out what my balance was and to find out what unknown charges they took out (i.e., my ATM card)—to see if I needed to call the bank and complain.

Djamaldin

During the week I've read the book *Forgotten Five,* which I enjoyed. My purpose for reading was to find out what is going to happen to the boy named Valian. Is he going to escape again or will he just stay a slave?

Olivia

This weekend I read my application packet and brochure for the college of my choice. My purpose in reading this was to find out the things I need to send them, or the deadlines, and to see their average freshman grades for the last year.

Amanda

This weekend I read a dream directory. My purpose for reading this was I have been having the same type of dreams lately, so I wanted to look up some of the things that I was dreaming about to see what they meant.

Steven

This weekend I read an article about a game online. My purpose for reading this was to learn about upcoming events in an online game I play.

Joseph

This weekend I read an installation guide for some software. The purpose for reading this was to find out how to install the software properly.

Kristen

This weekend I read my new issue of *Motor Trend* that I got in the mail. My purpose for reading this was to learn more about some of the new cars that are coming out in 2002 and some of the new concept cars I've heard about.

Rajah

This weekend I read an article about one of the shark attacks. My purpose was to better understand how doctors can take a bit-off arm and put it back on.

Brad

This weekend I read help wanted ads. My purpose for reading was to see what kind of jobs were out there for me when I get out of high school. I was looking for something I could do, and how much they paid.

Zahra

This weekend I read the article on Pakistan women in the *Denver Post.* My purpose was to see what they said about how women get treated. I always wonder what they can and can't do.

Chris

This weekend I read the Applebee's menu. My purpose for reading this was to find something good to get my grub on with. (Southwestern steak if you want to know.) I looked for things I liked, and if I didn't like it, I didn't read it.

Ashley

This weekend I read over my script before curtain call. My purpose for reading my script over was because I was nervous. Although I had my lines memorized, I wanted to make sure so I read over them again before my cue to go on stage.

some teachers new to the profession. Molly, a third-year teacher, said she was really struggling with her tenth graders. I asked her what they were reading, and she said *A Prayer for Owen Meany*. Confident in my quick assessment of the problem, I replied: "Molly, that's the problem. *Owen Meany* is a really tough book. Maybe it is too hard for your students and you should use an easier text."

Molly said, "No, the kids aren't the ones with the problem. They are doing fine on the quizzes and assignments. I am the one with the problem. This is the third time that I've used this book, and every time I read it with a class, I have more and more trouble. It seems to get harder to teach."

Now I was thoroughly confused. Each time I teach something, it gets easier, not harder. So I probed, "Molly, tell me what's hard."

"Well, the first time I used the book, there were only a few things I wanted the kids to know. The second time I taught the book, there were a few more things I wanted students to know about, but I managed to get it all in. This third time around, there is so much in the book that I need to teach that I don't know what to leave in and what to take out."

Molly's problem was clear. She was becoming an expert reader of *A Prayer for Owen Meany*. She had read it six times. She had read literary criticism about it as well as biographical information about the author, John Irving. She had discussed the novel with colleagues who had also used it with students. Molly knew the book so well that she was having trouble deciding what to teach and what to leave out.

This is a common problem for teachers. Many of us become experts on our content. We become familiar with our textbooks and novels and often forget what it was like to be a beginning student of our disciplines. Inadvertently, we water down our content because we try to cover too much.

One of my biggest challenges is helping content teachers identify a clear instructional purpose for assigned reading. When I meet with teachers of different content areas in workshops, I often have them work together to narrow down their purposes for a specific text. I use the instructional focus guide sheet to help them focus their thinking. A copy of the guide sheet is in the appendix.

For example, Laura is a Spanish teacher who struggles to balance instruction around grammar, literary elements, information about Spanish-speaking countries, and new vocabulary (see Figure 5.2). She anticipates that as students read the next chapter in their Spanish textbook, they might struggle with new vocabulary, a new verb tense, and the fact that they have little background knowledge about Puerto Rico. Laura decides to tackle the verb tense, because understanding tense will be essential for understanding the chapter. She will help students discover that there are patterns in Spanish, just like in English. She will show this by demonstrating what she does when she comes to unknown or new words. It's important to her that she show students strategies other than just using the dictionary.

Figure 5.2 Instructional Purposes—Spanish

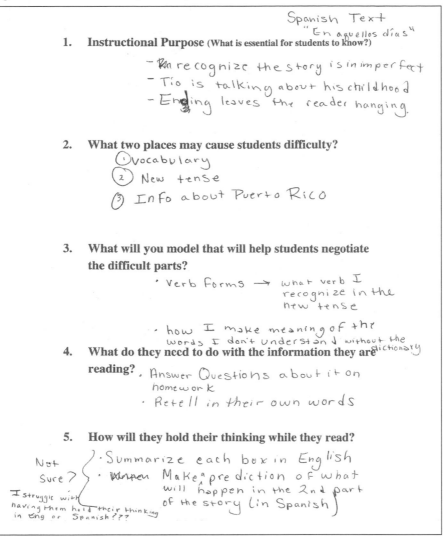

She admits that she struggles with the "holding thinking" aspect of strategy instruction work. I suggest that she have students use sticky notes to summarize in their own words what they have read. The summary should be short. Students could then in get in small groups and share their sticky notes. This would give them an opportunity to talk about the reading and encourage them to reread parts of the text.

Amy, a science teacher, uses the instructional focus sheet to narrow down the topic of cloning in the article she has copied for students to read (see Figure 5.3).

Figure 5.3 Instructional Purposes—Science

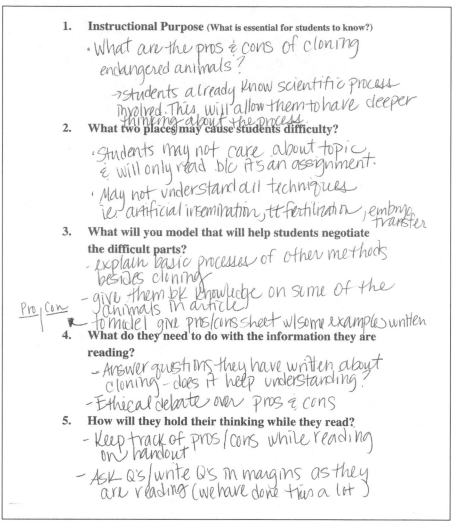

1. **Instructional Purpose** (What is essential for students to know?)

    • What are the pros & cons of cloning endangered animals?

    → students already know scientific process involved. This will allow them to have deeper thinking about the process.

2. **What two places may cause students difficulty?**

    • Students may not care about topic & will only read b/c it's an assignment.

    • May not understand all techniques ie. artificial insemination, tt fertilization, embryo transfer

3. **What will you model that will help students negotiate the difficult parts?**

    – explain basic processes of other methods besides cloning

    – give them bk knowledge on some of the animals in article

    Pro/Con – to model give pros/cons sheet w/some examples written

4. **What do they need to do with the information they are reading?**

    – Answer questions they have written about cloning – does it help understanding?

    – Ethical debate over pros & cons

5. **How will they hold their thinking while they read?**

    – Keep track of pros/cons while reading on handout

    – Ask Q's/write Q's in margins as they are reading (we have done this a lot)

She decides to focus her struggling readers' attention on the pros and cons of genetically engineered endangered animals. Amy anticipates that her students may not care about the topic enough to read through the entire article. She decides to create curiosity by building some background knowledge for the students and explains a few key terms: artificial insemination, fertilization, and embryo transfer.

I suggest that Amy give the students opportunities to ask questions. If she records their questions, she can use them to build reasons for the reading. Amy can also ask questions as a way to guide students' learning and to model the fact

Figure 5.4 Instructional Purposes—Math

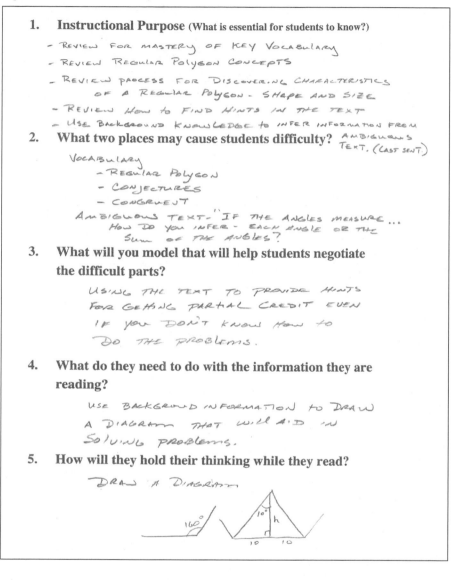

1. **Instructional Purpose** (What is essential for students to know?)
   - REVIEW FOR MASTERY OF KEY VOCABULARY
   - REVIEW REGULAR POLYGON CONCEPTS
   - REVIEW PROCESS FOR DISCOVERING CHARACTERISTICS
        OF A REGULAR POLYGON - SHAPE AND SIZE
   - REVIEW HOW to FIND HINTS IN THE TEXT
   - USE BACKGROUND KNOWLEDGE to INFER INFORMATION FROM

2. **What two places may cause students difficulty?** AMBIGUOUS TEXT. (LAST SENT.)

   VOCABULARY
      - REGULAR POLYGON
      - CONJECTURES
      - CONGRUENT
   AMBIGUOUS TEXT- "IF THE ANGLES MEASURE ...
        HOW DO YOU INFER - EACH ANGLE OR THE
          SUM OF THE ANGLES?

3. **What will you model that will help students negotiate the difficult parts?**

   USING THE TEXT TO PROVIDE HINTS
   FOR GETTING PARTIAL CREDIT EVEN
   IF YOU DON'T KNOW HOW to
   DO THE PROBLEMS.

4. **What do they need to do with the information they are reading?**

   USE BACKGROUND INFORMATION to DRAW
   A DIAGRAM THAT WILL AID IN
   SOLVING PROBLEMS.

5. **How will they hold their thinking while they read?**

   DRAW A DIAGRAM

that scientists wonder. Amy decides to have students mark their questions in the margin of the text as they read. She will record the questions after the class is finished reading, and then use them to guide the rest of the unit on cloning.

   Jim, a math teacher, prepares his students for a test (Figure 5.4). He uses the instructional focus sheet to identify key vocabulary and concepts. He anticipates that students will struggle with the ambiguous text in the math textbook. He knows that students probably won't know they have to infer each angle or the sum of the angles. Jim decides to help them negotiate this difficulty by referring students to the text, and pointing out parts that will give them clues for partial credit. I suggest he model this for the class, using a different problem or section of the textbook. Jim decides that students will also need to hold their thinking by drawing diagrams while reading.

When teachers take the time to think through the questions on the instructional focus sheet, they realize they can usually eliminate several components of their planned instruction because they distract students from the core objectives. It is not up to me or any other outsider to tell teachers what to teach and what to skip when using any text. Those decisions need to be made at the local level.

The instructional focus sheet is just a tool to help teachers think through what is most essential. We must start with the essential and then add the details. The first time I taught world literature, I didn't know very much about the content and worked hard to learn it. I read all summer long, preparing for the course. I read not only the anthology, but all the literary criticism I could find on the pieces of literature we would read in the fall. Each time I taught the class, I improved. I saw more connections to history and geographic settings, and I became more knowledgeable.

Who's In Charge of Setting Curriculum?

It's funny that we don't ask of ourselves what we ask of our students. When we are planning a unit, preparing to teach a new class, or picking up a textbook for the very first time, we don't expect to master everything in a semester. Yet we expect our students to master the information in less time than we the experts did.

I sympathize with history teachers. It seems that they have unbelievable amounts of content to cover. I am forever harping on our history teachers to cut out some of their content, so that students have time to slow down and think about what they are learning. They tell me that they have to cover certain eras.

One year, I finally asked some U.S. history teachers at my high school to tell me the time periods that were required. They told me they must begin at the pre-Columbian era and end with modern day. I asked them who told them where to begin and end. They stammered, and then told me our principal had told them.

One day I asked our principal, Jeannine, "Do U.S. history teachers really have to begin with the pre-Columbian era and go through modern day?"

She replied, "What is the pre-Columbian era?"

I told her that I thought it was the time in North America before Columbus's arrival, and that I guessed it meant that you would teach about Native Americans. A former math teacher, she replied, "I don't care where they start. They're the experts of their content. They should be the ones deciding where to begin."

I returned to the group of history teachers with the happy news: "Jeannine doesn't care where you guys start! You don't have to begin with the pre-Columbian era!" I expected rejoicing, but instead they told me that if she hadn't mandated it, it must have been mandated by the district social studies coordinator.

When I called him that afternoon, the district social studies coordinator told me there wasn't a district-mandated starting point. I then called area high schools and asked where they began their U.S. history curriculum. Each one began in a different era.

I finally called the state department of education to see what they recommended. Their response was that each high school student in Colorado is required to take a U.S. history class and a civics class. Beyond that baseline requirement, it is up to each district or school to decide what is taught. At that point I realized that "they" is often "us" when it comes to mandates about content.

If we don't help students pull out essential information by giving them a purpose for their reading, they will often get lost in the extraneous details. When we share a clear instructional purpose, we give our students a lens through which to read the piece.

For example, a U.S. history teacher may say to his students, "By the time you finish reading tonight, I want you to be able to discuss three causes of the Civil War." The teacher is not telling students the causes; he is merely giving them a sense of what will be important for tomorrow's discussion.

Clear instructional purposes often give guidance for how the reader might hold her thinking. Perhaps sticky notes placed inside the text highlighting causes of the Civil War would be a good match for the purpose assigned by the teacher.

In a science class where the teacher is asking students to recognize the first five phases of mitosis, a double-entry diary with a sketch of the mitotic phase on the left-hand side and the characteristics of the phase on the right-hand side might be the best way to hold thinking. A clear instructional purpose can greatly improve a reader's comprehension, because the reader has an indication of what to read for.

What Is Your Instructional Purpose?

1. Decide what students should know after reading the piece. Focus on essential information only.
2. Anticipate what might cause students difficulty.
   Are students lacking background knowledge?
   Will difficult vocabulary interfere with meaning?
   Will difficult concepts need to be explained further?
   Is the text about challenging subject matter?
   Is the text organized in a confusing manner?
3. Model how you would negotiate difficulty. Try thinking out loud at one of the places where you anticipate students will experience difficulty. Give them a tip on how to negotiate the next part.
4. What do you want them to be able to do with the information once they have finished reading? How will they hold their thinking so they can return to it later to use in a discussion, a paper, or a project?
5. Model how they should hold their thinking and provide tools. Should they mark text, use sticky notes, complete a double-entry diary?

When I first started teaching, I didn't play fair. I would ask my students to read a novel. When they finished, I would ask them to go back and do something with the reading. Sometimes I would ask them to write a character sketch, or I might ask them to demonstrate how the main character changed from the beginning of the book to the end of the book. I shouldn't have been surprised by poorly written papers. Few if any of the kids went back and reread the novel looking for character changes. Those who actually read the book most likely read it for the plot. That's how I typically read a book the first time—I try to follow the action. With subsequent readings, I begin to notice nuances of the language and changes in characters.

To ask students to do something on a first read that we ourselves aren't doing is asking too much. If we recognize the fact that many students aren't going to reread the text, perhaps it would be more efficient to tell them up front what we want them to do with the information when they finish reading.

Some teachers think that setting a purpose limits the scope of the students' reading—that it dumbs down the work and makes it too easy on the kids. I agree that I am limiting the scope of student reading, but I don't agree that I am constraining their learning. When I read new text with unfamiliar content, I need my scope limited. If it's not limited, I try to remember everything in the text. I quickly realize that I can't do this and soon give up. When someone gives me something to look for, reading feels less overwhelming.

Adults who are learning a new skill or preparing to enter a new profession are told what they need to know. My sister-in-law recently got her realtor's license. She was told what she needed to know to pass the test. This helped her to read, study, and memorize what was most essential. Certainly she will keep learning more about real estate as she grows in her profession and experiences more real estate deals. Thankfully, there is a little book that tells drivers what they need to know to get a driver's license. As they gain experience driving, they gain additional information about what it means to be a good driver.

Doctors are given a baseline of information of what they need to know, as are lawyers and stockbrokers. If these professionals are given a lens through which to learn about their fields, shouldn't we do the same for our students?

There are a lot of things that we as teachers can't control. But we can control what we ask our kids to do with the information we assign.

What Do Readers Do When They Aren't Given a Purpose?

Recently I was encouraging teachers at a summer institute to find engaging, accessible text for students to read. All of a sudden, an arm attached to a gruff-looking principal shot up into the air. Before I could call on him, he started to talk. "Interesting and well-written text is fine, but what are teachers supposed to use for students planning on attending college? Everyone knows that college students and even adults have to read boring, difficult text."

He had a point. In the real world, readers are expected to read all types of text. As a teacher, I am often asked to read dry, difficult text that holds little interest for me. However, I don't read every piece of boring text that crosses my desk. Much of it goes unread and into the trash can. I don't arbitrarily throw it away; I have a specialized screening process. For me to spend time getting through a piece of uninteresting, ho-hum text, I must have a purpose. I must have a reason for reading the piece. There must be something in it that will make my life as a teacher or a person better. If the piece isn't going to entertain, teach, or improve my life in some way, I throw it out.

The same is true for our students. If they don't see how the piece is going to improve their life in some small way, they will have difficulty getting through it. Sometimes our students can't see the importance of something that we ask them to read. They may just need to read the piece to pass the test. Sometimes we have to read something we don't want to in order to keep our job, or we may have to read and understand something so that we don't get cheated.

My former principal often put articles in my box that I wouldn't normally read on my own. At the top of the article, she would write, *What do you think?* I couldn't anticipate her position, so I wasn't sure how to respond. I knew she would call me into her office to talk about the article. Sooner or later I would have to read it. Often the pieces were boring, but if I wanted to look good in front of my boss, I had to read the article and be able to share some thinking about it.

I realize that no one now gives me a purpose for most of the reading I do. I have to give myself a

> ### Determining Possible Purposes
>
> Decide how you will *hold your thinking* as you read. What does the teacher want you to do with the information? Maybe your purpose is to answer questions or write an essay later. What thinking do you need to hold?
>
> 1. Look for *interesting details* that could have multiple meanings. Ask yourself, "Why did the author or cartoonist add that detail?"
> 2. Ask questions about the *title and subtitle.* Try to figure out how the title and subtitle are connected to the piece.
> 3. Ask questions about the *piece.* As you read, record the questions and keep them in the back of your mind. Look for the answers as you read. If you don't find the answers, ask the questions the next day in class.
> 4. Look for the author's *opinion.* Compare his or her opinion with your own. Does the author agree or disagree with you?
> 5. Read a piece to learn *new information.* Is there anything in the reading that helps you understand the topic better?
> 6. Make a *connection* to the piece. Does the piece remind you of an experience, a movie, or information you already know? Does the connection help you relate to a person or situation? Use information you have about the topic to connect more personally to the piece.
> 7. Who is the *author*? Do you know anything about the author and his or her style of writing? Is he or she sarcastic or serious? Is he or she politically conservative or liberal? What you know about the author might help you anticipate what is coming in the reading.

purpose if I am to remember what I've read. When I read a challenging piece, asking questions often pulls me through it. I begin right at the title, marking my questions directly on the text. If I am reading a contract or a textbook that I can't write on, I write my questions on sticky notes and attach them to the margins next to the words that cause me to have the question. I ask questions that directly affect me—questions I truly care about. The questions I ask propel me to read on to find my answer. If my questions aren't answered in the text, they are held in the margins to discuss later.

There is a direct translation from this process to classroom instruction. When students perceive a piece to be boring or difficult, setting a purpose will help them through the read. Not long ago my senior English students asked me what they should do when they have a teacher who doesn't give them a purpose for their reading. We began to generate a list of possible purposes that they could set for themselves as they read (see the list on the previous page).

I hesitated to put this list in the book. My fear is it will be used as a checklist, and that students will be asked to read for all of these purposes with a single piece of text. The intention of this list is to give readers some options by which to read a difficult or boring piece.

How Do I Turn My Reciting Voice Off and My Conversation Voice On?

Many times when students don't have a purpose for their reading, their minds wander. Early in the year, I explain to my students that when I read, I hear voices, one of which is the sound of me reading the words. I call it my reciting voice. It's the voice that reads the words but thinks about other things. When this voice is on, I don't remember what I've read. My other voice is my conversation voice. It's the sound of me talking back to the text. Sometimes this voice argues with the author, or makes a connection to what the author is saying. Sometimes this voice asks questions or agrees with what the author is saying.

Recognizing that readers have different voices when they read is a powerful monitoring device. If students can learn to recognize the difference between their reciting voice and their conversation voice, they will know when they are no longer making sense of the text. I find that if the text is difficult and the content is unfamiliar, readers have a tendency to read the words with their reciting voice. They blast through the text, only to find they don't remember a word they read.

Toward the end of the year, Lyndsay, a bright ninth grader, helped me understand a new role for setting a purpose in reading. One day she wrote in a note to me, "When I read social studies, my reciting voice is on. When we get to the part about the wars, my conversation voice turns on. How do I turn my reciting voice off and my conversation voice on when I am just reading normal social studies?" Her question told me that she was beginning to take control of her reading.

Lyndsay recognized the different voices in her head. She knew that when her reciting voice was on, she wasn't constructing meaning, and that when that voice came on, she became disinterested in the text. Lyndsay also knew that when her conversation voice was on, she remembered what she read and was more interested in the text. The question is, How do we help Lyndsay and students like her keep their conversation voices on? I think it comes down to setting a purpose.

Last fall, as the United States' involvement in the Middle East escalated, I decided it was important for my students to become more aware of what was going on, so that they could make connections to their history coursework. I came across some letters to the editor in a copy of *Time* magazine and decided to have the students read one of them in class, which would give them some information to generate a lively discussion. The next day, we read a short letter, and I asked students to begin talking about their opinions.

My second-hour class was rarely at a loss for words, but they were silent. They were clearly not interested in the piece. They read the letter to the editor, but they read it with their reciting voice. After a bit of probing, I realized that the majority of the class didn't understand the purpose of letters to editors. I had to revise my lesson—I had to figure out how to turn their reciting voices off and their conversation voices on. The only way to do this was to give them a purpose for the reading.

> **The Good and Bad "Voices" Readers Hear**
>
> Students can be taught to distinguish between the "voices in their head" while reading. Here are some distinctions to discuss with students:
>
> *Reciting voice:* The voice readers hear when they are only reciting the words and not drawing meaning from the text.
>
> *Conversation voice:* The voice that has a conversation with the text. It represents the readers' thinking as they talk back to the text. This voice can take two forms:
>
> > *Interacting voice:* The voice inside the reader's head that makes connections, asks questions, identifies confusions, agrees and disagrees with ideas. This voice deepens the reader's understanding of the text.
> >
> > *Distracting voice:* The voice inside the reader's head that pulls her away from the meaning of the text. It begins a conversation with the reading but gets distracted by a connection, a question, or an idea. Soon the reader begins to think about something unrelated to the text.
>
> *Adapted from Tovani 2000*

That evening I sat down and asked myself, "Why do I read letters to the editor?" Seeing others' opinions informs my thinking and helps me consider alternative viewpoints. I know I don't have to agree with the author; it's okay to have a differing opinion. I realized that I had assumed that my students had similar purposes while reading.

I designed a comprehension constructor (see Figure 5.5). At the top, I put a few lines with a prompt that would help students state an initial opinion. Next, I left a space for them to write down what they thought the author's opinion was. The final third of the sheet had a place for students to compare the two opinions. I was pretty confident that after going through this process, students would have a bit of knowledge about how to read a letter to the editor, they would know more about the United States' involvement in the Middle East, and they would be better prepared to share their thinking with peers.

Figure 5.5 Letter to the Editor Comprehension Constructor

Name: _____

Purpose: Comparing your opinion to the opinions of others.
Below are two letters to the editor. The people who wrote these letters have stated their opinions about the impending war with Iraq and have explained why they think the way they do. Do you think that the United States should attack Iraq?

In my opinion the United States _____

because _____

Read the letters below. Do the authors agree or disagree with you?
America's main intention in Iraq is self-preservation. U.S. taxpayers do not want to spend their hard-earned money on nation building. What we want and are entitled to is to go to sleep at night knowing that our children will not be wiped off the face of the earth by some maniac. Maybe we will fail in our nation building in Iraq, but at least we will eliminate one of our greatest threats. We hope the next Iraqi leader will be human. Let's roll the dice.
    Dan Dillulio
    Stamford, Conn.

If the goal of war against Iraq is to eliminate the threat of weapons of mass destruction ["Iraq: Weapons Inspections," Sept. 30], why not act against other nations that have them? If the goal is the liberation of the Iraqi people, then why aren't those who want war speaking up for other oppressed peoples of the world? The main U.S. objective is to install a friendly, puppet-like regime (probably not a democratic one, considering Iraq's past) that will greatly lessen U.S. dependence on Saudi oil and allow the U.S. to pressure Riyadh on its record of exporting terrorists.
    Gorm Bjorhovde
    Tromso, Norway

Thinking:

From Letters to the Editor. Time. October 28, 2002. Reprinted with permission.

Lyndsay had helped me see that when students aren't doing what I ask, there must be a reason. Sometimes the text is too difficult or the vocabulary is too complex, but that really wasn't the case with the letters to the editor. In this case I had not given students a purpose for the reading. They had no idea how they were supposed to think about the text.

I think it all comes down to trusting our content. U.S. history is fascinating—our engagement in war and connections to previous wars are inherently interesting to kids. Science is fascinating, and so is a beautifully constructed poem. But students will find their own connections to our content only if we teach them to read purposefully, talking back to the text and sorting through the information as they read.

What Works

1. Be selective about what kids read. If everything in the text isn't important or well written, don't assign it all. Sift out the best parts—it doesn't have to be all or nothing.

   Teaching Point: Good readers skip, skim, and scan text continually, based on their purpose. They also reread, slow down, and reread again if it suits their purpose.

2. Be specific about your instructional purpose. Give students a lens for reading the piece.

   Teaching Point: Good readers know a purpose will help them focus their reading and determine what is important. They also know that purpose determines how they read the material.

3. Decide how your students will use what they are reading. Explain to them how they will use the information when they are finished.

   Teaching Point: Good readers approach assigned text with a result in mind. They consider what they will have to do with the information after reading.

6

Holding Thinking to Remember and Reuse

I don't look at a book as a whole bunch of words. I look at it as someone's thinking, and the information the author wants me to know.

Brad, high school senior

On the first day of school, I begin the reading workshop class by showing a picture of a member of the Navy Seals climbing a rope ladder to a helicopter. Coming out of the water are the immense jaws of a great white shark just about to bite the man on the ladder. In the background are hills, and above the helicopter is the partial shot of a giant red metal bridge.

I show this picture to my students on the overhead and say, "What do you think?" At first no one says a word. One way to begin showing students different options for thinking about text is to start with a provocative picture. For students who struggle to read anything, the most accessible text is the one with the fewest possible words.

I keep repeating the question, "What do you think?" until someone gets sick of the wait time and responds.

Cameron says, "That is so fake."

Derrick responds, "Yeah, I agree. They probably did this with Photoshop."

Mallory counters, "I wonder if it's real. Look at the words above the picture." The words read, "This is a real photo. It was taken in South African waters of British Navy Seals doing a water rescue drill. This photo has been nominated as *National Geographic*'s Photo of the Year."

"See," says Mallory. "The words say that it's a real photo."

"So what? That doesn't mean it's true," snaps Aaron.

"I used to live in California, and that bridge looks like the Golden Gate Bridge—which is in San Francisco, not South Africa," says Mike.

The room becomes quiet as the class considers what has been said. I take the photo off the overhead projector and put on a blank transparency. I start to write down all the types of thinking that I saw students engaging in as they examined the photo.

I say to the class, "Look what you guys did as you 'read' this picture. You questioned the validity of it. You asked questions. You made connections to what you know about the world. You were thinking as you read this piece. Whether you know it or not, you are thinking all the time. When you look at a picture or watch television, you are thinking. The type of thinking you did today is the same type of thinking you want to do when you read."

The students are right to question the photo. The picture is actually a hoax: two photos were spliced together and circulated on the Internet. *National Geographic News* even published an essay describing the hoax and the origin of the two pictures (Danielson 2002). You can also access the article at http://news.nationalgeographic.com/news/2002/08/0815_020815_photooftheyear.html.

I glance at the clock, and see that the bell is about to ring. "Tomorrow we will try this again with another piece of text."

I have helped students become aware that they are thinking even when "reading" a picture. My next step is to help them learn different ways of holding their thinking while reading text.

Time for Thinking

It takes time to teach kids how to share their thinking about a piece of text, and it can be frustrating at first. But this idea that thinking while reading has to be made visible or held in some way is very important. Thinking while reading is difficult to measure because it's so complex, and it's invisible. You can see a kid's writing and you can see a kid work a math problem. But this idea that we can see students make sense of text is impossible to document unless they can talk about it or respond to it artistically or write about it in some way.

The concept of holding and marking thinking is new to a lot of students, because they've been taught that it's the teacher's job to ask the questions, and the student's job to answer them. But when I'm trying to learn something new in the real world, I'm the one asking the questions. That is what I try to replicate in the classroom, regardless of the content students are trying to master.

When students find ways to capture their thinking while reading, they are more willing to return to texts. They tend to participate more in classroom discussions as well as in small-group discussions. They have an easier time beginning writing assignments. The marked text gives them a way to review and study for a test.

I often work with teachers who are just beginning to teach their students how to mark text. They are sometimes on the verge of giving up because their students struggle to write anything at first, and the thinking they do mark on sticky notes or in the margins of text is so weak. These teachers think that their kids aren't cognitively ready to do this "high school" activity.

The problem has nothing to do with age or cognitive readiness. First graders can hold thinking with great success if they are taught how to do it. My students also struggle at first, and some still struggle late in the year. Kids need a lot of time to practice, but they also need tangible models that show them what we expect. Sometimes the models come from the work of their classmates.

Mark Twain once said, "No one is smart enough to remember all that he knows." When I don't have a way to hold my thinking while reading challenging texts, I often have trouble remembering or returning to my reading. No matter how hard I try to remember my thinking as I read, I forget it if I don't have a way to make it permanent. I especially struggle to remember the reading if it is difficult or boring. I find that the same is true for my students.

I have to teach students how to show their thinking again and again. It doesn't miraculously happen because I've assigned it. When I first begin teaching students different ways to show me their understanding, very little shows up on the page for many of them. Discussions in small groups or with the whole class are brief and awkward.

I want kids to follow certain guidelines when marking text. This is what I ask of them:

- Write the thinking next to the words on the page that cause you to have the thought.
- If there isn't room on the text to write, draw a line showing the teacher where the thinking is written.
- Don't copy the text; respond to it.
- Merely underlining text is not enough. Thinking about the text must accompany the underlining.
- There is no one way to respond to text. Here are some possible options: Ask a question, make a connection to something familiar, give an opinion, draw a conclusion, make a statement.

Some of these points seem obvious to us as adults, but I find that if I am not explicit about what I want, I don't get what I want. Because it is new to students, we have to spend a lot of time and energy on a small amount of text. Yet it is worth the time and effort. Thinking held on paper not only informs our instruc-

---

Getting Students Started with Marking Text

1. Mark one quote in the text, and have a conversation about the quote.
2. Write a question that doesn't have a simple answer.
3. Ask your partner's opinion about your ideas.
4. Are you copying information from the text or sharing your thinking? Share thinking!
5. Make a statement or recommendation, based on what you've read. Don't be wishy-washy.

tion and can be used as an alternative assessment tool for a more accurate picture of student learning, but also helps students rehearse their thinking before they begin a writing assignment.

Moving from Pictures to Text

On the second day of school, students in my reading workshop come in hoping to look at more shark pictures. Much to their chagrin, they find a short article waiting for each of them on their desks. The article is from the local newspaper, about a controversy in a small town near our high school. A twelve-year-old girl has gone to court for an overdue library book. She has been put on probation and has had to pay a fine. It is difficult for anyone to read the article and not have some emotional reaction.

I ask the kids to read the piece and try to record at least two pieces of thinking in the margin. Each piece of thinking is worth five points. There is no right answer—the only way they can fail is if they don't write anything down. I am not looking for anything specific. At this point in the year, I've done little to explain my point or evaluation system. The key idea is that they have to record some thinking to receive credit.

As the students read, I circulate, trying to see who has decoding issues, who hates to read, who is engaged, and who can comprehend. For many students, it takes the entire period to read and write.

That afternoon after students have left for the day, I go through the pieces and make overheads of four or five examples to show the class the next day. I use student examples in a positive way throughout the year to point out what students are doing well. Many times peer examples are more effective than adult examples. This technique is also a good way to honor kids' thinking and to begin rebuilding shattered self-esteem for struggling readers.

The next morning I pass back the graded articles about the twelve-year-old with an overdue book. The examples that I have chosen are not stellar, but they are all I've got. I explain to the class that I want them to see some examples of good thinking. I start with Zach's response to the article by putting a copy of it on the overhead projector. On the right-hand side of the text he has written, "Oh well, it's not my problem."

I point out that Zach has done something good readers do. He has decided that this piece has no relevance to his life. Not the most profound thinking, but I am validating Zach's right to not be engaged in everything he reads.

Next, I put up Brandon's piece. Initially he had just underlined words. As the class was reading I was circulating the room, touching base with individual students the day before, I had pointed out to Brandon that I could tell he thought his underlined words were important. But because I couldn't read his mind, he would have to write and tell me his thoughts about the underlined words. Brandon drew a line from the words on the page that he had underlined and wrote, "I was thinking that she had just blown off the notices and didn't care about them."

I point out to the class that Brandon too has done something good readers do. He has made an inference. He has taken statements from the text and used his background knowledge to interpret those statements to draw a conclusion.

I continue putting examples on the overhead. Zipping through them, I accidentally put up Aaron's paper. His example was not meant to be shared with this class. I had made a copy to share with a group of teachers in other content areas with whom I would meet later that afternoon. They were discouraged that their student work wasn't very good early in the year, as they were just introducing students to different ways of marking thinking as they read textbooks.

I had decided I would show them some student examples from the first week of class, and then show them examples several months down the road so they could see how the thinking and writing improved as students became more comfortable with the strategies and expectations.

But by the time I realize my mistake of putting up Aaron's paper, it is too late to take it off the overhead projector. The class has already seen that it is his, and they want to know why I have selected it.

Aaron is a big kid: six feet tall and not even fourteen years old. He weighs close to two hundred pounds and is as tough as nails. The first day of class he came up and stood toe to toe with me as he announced, "I don't read and nobody is gonna make me." Aaron has come to my school from South Central Los Angeles, and has fought his way through every other school he has attended.

Pulling his paper off the overhead without discussing it will cause questions and break any trust I hope to build with Aaron. I decide to improvise some learning from what he has written. I show the class that although there is no writing on the top, bottom, or left-hand margin of the paper, there is writing on the bottom right-hand side. Aaron has written, "I did not write anything."

When I had first read this comment while grading papers the night before, my reaction was, "Fine, you want to play this game? I can play this game too. Here's a big fat zero for your grade." Thankfully I didn't follow my first instincts. I didn't know how to respond to his work, so I hadn't put any grade on his paper at all. I decided that I would talk to Aaron privately and see if he had reasons for not writing anything down. Putting his paper on the overhead wasn't the private conversation I had imagined. I forged on.

"What can we tell about Aaron's thinking?" I ask the class.

PJ, who is about half the size of Aaron, says, "Well, it's obvious he didn't read the article."

Aaron stands up, shoves his desk out of the way, walks over to PJ, and says, "The hell I didn't."

Tips for Students: Getting "Unstuck"

1. Trust the author. Don't panic if at first the text doesn't make sense. The author will slowly reveal clues.
2. Ask questions. Quite likely someone else may have the same question. Someone else may be able to clear up the confusion.
3. Slow down. Give yourself time to read, reread, and paraphrase what you've read.
4. It's okay to go back. Sometimes readers go back and reread confusing parts of texts.

Afraid that a fight is going to break out and that PJ is going to get hurt, I try to distract Aaron. "Wait a second, Aaron." I turn to PJ. "You know, PJ, I believe that Aaron read the article."

Wide-eyed and pale, PJ says, "You do?"

"Sure I do. The problem, though," I say as I turn to Aaron and try to motion him back into his seat, "is that I can't read your mind and you haven't written anything down. I can't see your thinking. Aaron, if you want to look at the rest of the examples I put on the overhead and listen in on the conversation, you might have some thinking to add. If you do, mark it down and turn your paper into the basket for more points." Aaron doesn't say a word, but I can tell he is considering the offer.

I move on. Quickly. I put up David's example, in which he has just copied the text word for word. I point out that I almost missed his best thinking because he wrote it on the back of the page, which I then flip over for them to read. I tell the class that copying from the article is boring to read. What I am really interested in is their thoughts about it. I work hard to help them understand that there is not one right answer when thinking about a piece of text. If they become stuck in their reading, there are ways to get "unstuck."

That evening I go through the basket of student work from the morning. Aaron has turned in a second draft of his thinking. In the place where the article describes the details of the overdue book, Aaron writes, "That librarian must have been obsessed with books. . . . I'd be selling them." In the place where Marisa says she would be scared to check out another book, Aaron writes, "Why? She could of egged the place." In the place where he originally wrote, "I didn't write anything," he had erased his words and written, "Erased" (see Figure 6.1).

Aaron's final response perplexed me. I couldn't tell if he was teasing me or was really serious. I finally came to the conclusion that one of two things was going on in Aaron's head: (1) He thought I was the dumbest human being alive or (2) He was extremely literal and wanted to be sure that I knew he had gone back and shared more thinking. I choose to believe option 2.

Often students' struggles can be explained if we take the time to look at them closely, says Mike Rose in *Lives on the Boundary.*

Every day in our schools and colleges young people face reading and writing tasks that seem hard or unusual, that confuse them, that they fail. But if you can get close enough to their failure, you'll find knowledge that the assignment didn't tap, ineffective rules and strategies that have a logic of their own. (1990, p. 8)

Figure 6.1 Littleton Library *Denver Post* Article

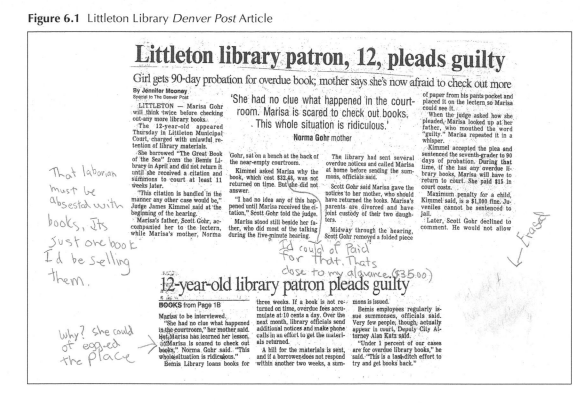

Part of my job early in the year is to get to know my students well enough to understand the logic behind what they do. As the year progressed, I confirmed my conclusion about Aaron: he was not a risk taker. He didn't want to be teased. It was easier for him to be thought of as lazy than as stupid. Aaron was a literal reader. If it wasn't in black and white, right in front of him, it didn't exist. Aaron turned in every assignment that year—not always on time, but he turned them in. When he didn't turn something in, it was a signal that he didn't know what to do and needed more modeling or explanation. Once Aaron knew what to do, the work appeared. Often his thinking was provocative and caused his classmates to delve deeper into the text.

Richard Vacca said something at the 2003 International Reading Association conference in the opening keynote talk that reminded me of Aaron. He said, "All struggling readers have to do is act tough and then say nothing, and they can become invisible." That is what Aaron had tried to do. The first day of school, he tried to intimidate me by saying he didn't read and no one was going

> **Possible Uses of Sticky Notes**
>
> When students can't write on the text, sticky notes make it possible to still mark thinking there. Sticky notes can flag a page and mark a line so readers can
>
> - find a part quickly;
> - mark a confusing part to get clarification;
> - hold thinking to share later.

Possible Uses of Highlighters

Suggestion: Photocopy a short piece of text, a page from the textbook or novel, a graph or a word problem. Make a transparency, and model places in the text where you highlight. Give students an opportunity to do the same. Use highlighted students' sheets to drive the discussion.

- Give students a yellow highlighter to mark places that are confusing, and a pink highlighter to mark places that they understand well enough to explain to someone else in the class.
- Use any color highlighter to emphasize the reader's purpose in the text. For example:
  a line that causes the reader to ask a question
  a line that the reader can personally relate to
  a line that strikes the reader
  a word or term that is unknown
  a section that is well written.

to make him do it. He sat in the back at first, and never participated in discussions. He truly did try to become invisible.

The question for me is, If students become invisible, does it mean we no longer have the responsibility to teach them? When I went back and looked at Aaron's middle school grades, I saw that he had failed almost every class but continued to move up through the grades. Is that how Aaron came to be a ninth grader barely able to read and write? He intimidated me and then acted as though he didn't care about the work. As a classroom teacher, it can be tempting to ignore failing students, to write them off as unwilling to try. Aaron would not have improved as a reader and writer if he had never had an opportunity to read and write. Sure, the work he is doing now isn't ninth-grade level, but it's better than when he started ninth grade. Teaching readers how to hold thinking allows them to participate in many ways, regardless of their skill level.

Tools for Holding Thinking

Where Am I Supposed to Get These Materials for Holding Thinking?

Add sticky notes and highlighters to students' supply list.

I ask that students bring in three packs of 2.5-by-2.5-inch sticky notes. They give me two and keep the third to use in their other classes.

I also ask half of my classes to bring in yellow highlighters and the other half to bring in pink highlighters. I keep the highlighters in baskets so they are always available.

I've never had anyone complain about bringing in the supplies. I mention that if this is a hardship on the family, it's not a problem. I keep a record of who brought in the supplies, which tends to propel students who "forget" to bring them in.

Highlighters get old after awhile. Sticky notes get old after awhile. Blown-up pieces of text on a bulletin board get old after awhile. Having a lot of different tools not only helps keep the interest high, but also helps kids have different options for remembering what they've read.

When you first start using highlighters, students will color everything on the page. Same thing with sticky notes—a few students will be writing phrases like "kick me" and sticking them on people. But that becomes old too, and students quickly start to use the tools more appropriately.

I try to be realistic. They are not going to use all of these tools when they leave my classroom. But if they leave knowing how to use sticky notes to hold their thinking when they are reading so that they have specific evidence from the text when they write a response, they have gained an important skill. Or if they leave knowing how to highlight text—not everything on the page, but the important information that will help them master some difficult content—I am happy with that.

Many times I have kids mark their thinking directly on the text. When students can't mark on their text, they can use sticky notes. Sometimes students turn in their books with sticky notes inside. Other times I ask students to remove their sticky notes, write the page number where the note was taken on each one, and attach them to a piece of notebook paper. Then I can grade the thinking or give credit for the reading without carrying thirty books home.

Whole-Group Thinking

Whole-group charts make class thinking public, and are very useful in getting students started with learning how to mark thinking in text. When some students are having difficulty seeing a strategy in use, I chart other students' thinking. Many times a student's words are just the ticket when it comes to helping another student understand what I mean.

I made a large copy of a short, interesting article on the Internet about how marketers target young drinkers. I modeled some of my thinking, and then had students read the article and write comments right on the page (see Figure 6.2).

On another day, I realized several kids were having trouble understanding what it meant to experience sensory images while reading. When I said, "Try to make a movie in your head when you read. Or notice the sounds you hear, or the smells you smell," they said, "What do you mean?" Many thought that there was one right picture, sound, or smell that they were supposed to get. They didn't understand that their past experiences would determine what the sensory images were.

Gary Paulsen's piece from *The Winter Room* called "Tuning" is great for demonstrating what I mean. I ask students to read the prologue and then highlight three places in the text where they can make a clear visual picture.

Next to the highlighted words, students describe the sensory images they are experiencing. Before class the next day, I chart examples from kids who need extra encouragement, and ones that exemplify use of the strategy. I put the readers' name next to the thinking and then share the chart with the class the next day (see Figure 6.3).

Comprehension Constructors

One of the terms I coined to describe teacher-designed tools that help students hold thinking is "comprehension constructors" (Tovani 2000). I thought of call-

Figure 6.2 Alcohol Chart Mark-Up

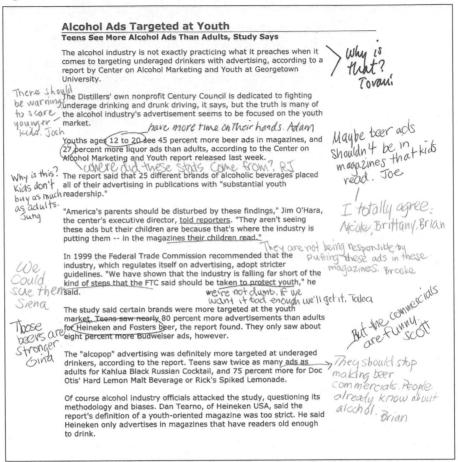

ing them "think sheets," but I discovered that someone else was using that term. And I certainly didn't want to describe them as worksheets, because that tends to imply one correct answer. Comprehension constructors are designed to pull kids through a comprehension process. I gave a few samples of these in my first book, and they proved to be one of its most popular features. Comprehension constructors help students name their thinking and make it visible. I've since rethought the design of any writing assignment that will be used when I want to help students understand content.

When I'm designing a comprehension constructor for students, I'm thinking about how I would read the piece and what I would need to do as a reader to get through it. Often I rely on one or two strategies more than others.

Figure 6.4 shows a couple of pages from a biology textbook used in our school. If I were going to design a comprehension constructor to help students

Figure 6.3 Understanding Sensory Images

"Tuning" from *The Winter Room* by Gary Paulsen
If books could be more, could show more, could own more, this book would have smells . . .

It would have the smells of old farms, the sweet smell of new-mown hay as it falls off the oiled sickle blade when the horses pull the mower through the field, and the sour smell of manure steaming in a winter barn. It would have the sticky-slick smell of birth when the calves come and they suck for the first time on the rich, new milk; the dusty smell of winter hay dried and stored in the loft waiting to be dropped down to the cattle; the pungent fermented smell of the chopped corn silage when it is brought into the manger on the silage fork.

Different sensory images we have created from the same piece of text:
I remember going to a carnival and seeing the petting zoo. I have the smell of the animals in my head when I read the part about the cows. *Erin*

When I get to the part where the horses are eating the grass, I smell the scent of grass that I get when I get tackled. *Ramel*

Every Saturday when the weather is nice my neighbor, Mr. Lee is mowing his lawn. Since my windows are open on nice days, I awaken to the sound of and smell of freshly mown grass. That's what I visual and smell when I read about the horses, cows and grass. *Yaneash*

When I read the part about the manure, I visual Biff from Back to the Future when he runs into the pile of manure. *Wayne*

I picture one of those old fashion mowers that have to be pushed. In my head it looks like the one I use at my grandpa's to mow his crab grass. *Matthew*

---

read this chapter on biological compounds, I would have to do several things. First, I would record my thinking on sticky notes as I read, to see where I get confused and need some help making sense of the text.

As I read, I would rely on two different thinking strategies. I would try to figure out how information in this chapter connects to previous chapters or what I already know about the topic. Looking at the title, the newly introduced vocabulary, and the graphics, I would want to know how they fit together. I would also try to connect terms and connect this new information to what I already know.

I would ask a lot of questions. Because it is in the book, I would assume the information is important, but I wouldn't know that for sure yet, because I'm not a biologist. An expert reader of this material could help me make connections if he or she could point out what is most essential for me to know right now.

With these concerns in mind, Figure 6.5 shows a comprehension constructor I might design to go with this text.

The comprehension constructor is a concrete way of taking students through an abstract process, and the simpler and more authentic it is, the better.

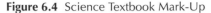

Figure 6.4 Science Textbook Mark-Up

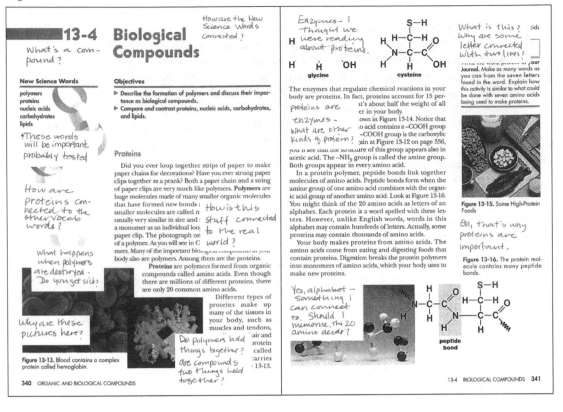

Whenever I work through a comprehension constructor with students, we talk about where else they can use the activity and thinking. How can you use it in science, in math, in your English class, your social studies class? I'm always trying to show them where it's useful. And I'm always trying to help them make a connection outside of my classes.

The biology textbook example would be challenging for many students, but even easily accessible texts can sometimes provoke more thinking when a comprehension constructor is designed to be used in tandem with them.

Designing comprehension constructors is a constant process of matching content, readers, and goals. In the following examples, I show how I and teachers I have worked with have come up with different designs to suit different learning goals.

Who Can Help You?

Recently I did a demonstration lesson in a chemistry class for students who weren't going to be science majors in college. The teacher complained that her

Figure 6.5 Science Textbook Comprehension Constructor

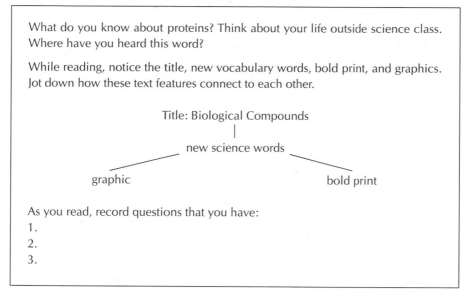

What do you know about proteins? Think about your life outside science class. Where have you heard this word?

While reading, notice the title, new vocabulary words, bold print, and graphics. Jot down how these text features connect to each other.

Title: Biological Compounds

new science words

graphic   bold print

As you read, record questions that you have:
1.
2.
3.

students were not reading actively. She had found a human-interest article in the newspaper that she thought would build background knowledge for the next unit of study. The article was about phosphate poisoning caused by tainted blue jeans that had been sold to immigrants at a discount price.

In years past, students would not read the article and therefore didn't have the information they needed to understand the chemical properties discussed in the next chapter of the textbook.

At the beginning of the demonstration, I shared with the class that good readers ask questions when they read. Leo asked, "What if I don't have any questions?"

I said, "I bet you will, but just in case you don't, here are some of the things I was wondering about." I put my list of questions on the transparency and began reading them. Leo stopped me.

"Well, of course you have questions about chemistry. You're an English teacher."

Leo was a student in my English class, so he knew that math and science were not my strong suits. "So you're saying that experts of topics don't have questions?"

Leo thought a moment and then said, "Yeah, this article looks easy. I probably won't have any questions because I do pretty well in here, and I know a lot about what we're talking about."

"Do you think your teacher Ms. Sengsvath knows a lot about the topic?"

"Sure," said Leo.

"Do you think she will have any questions?"

"Probably not."

Figure 6.6 Leo's Comprehension Constructor

Question I asked that I can answer after reading the article:	Question my teacher could answer if I asked:	Question I can answer myself by inferring:
Question: How ~~did~~ the poison get onto the jeans? Answer: From a leeckage of a phosphate in a semitruck while in the road.	Question: What is a phosphate? Answer: Mrs. Sengsavath	Question: Why were jeans in with the chemricals? Answer: maybe the a little room was left & they did not want to get another truck out.

Question I asked that I can answer after reading the article:	Question my teacher could answer if I asked:	Question I can answer myself by inferring:
Question: what is with the blue jeans? Answer: They have been contaminated.	Question: Is it legal to buy jeans off-hired hands? Answer: Mrs. Tovani	Question: why did the truckers sell the jeans? Answer: maybe to earn a little bit of extra cash.

"Hmmm." I turned to Debbie, the science teacher, and asked, "Ms. Sengsvath, by any chance did you have any questions while you were reading the article?"

"Funny you should ask," she said. "I do have questions." She removed my transparency of questions and added her list to the overhead. Because of her expertise, her list of questions was even longer than mine. Because she is an expert, her questions were also more sophisticated. Debbie and I compared the list of questions, pointing out that asking questions is a signal that you are constructing meaning. Readers who don't ask questions are often disengaged and unable to remember what they've read.

We pointed out that we also want them to find answers to their questions. The first step was to read the article and jot down in the margins any questions that arose. When students finished, they were to go back to the text and circle four or five questions that they liked the best. Next, students used the comprehension constructor called My Answer (see Figure 6.6). A blank copy can be found in the appendix.

Notice how Leo is able to flesh out his clarifying questions. He is also able to participate more in the reading because he is forced to infer answers to complex questions. Leo also sees that his teachers can provide some information that would clear up his confusion quickly.

Double-Strategy, Double-Entry Diary

Many students complain that they don't have any connections to a topic. The following example of a double-strategy, double-entry diary can be used with any content area (see Figure 6.7). The examples are from three different classes. The first one is from a science class that was reading a *Scientific American*

Figure 6.7 Double-Strategy, Double-Entry Examples

The Long Arm of the Immune System

Quote from article	Connection to Quote
1. Title	1. I've heard dendrites can be built by learning new tasks.
2. ...basis for all vaccines	2. Vaccines inject the disease into the person & the person builds up immune system.
3. ...white blood cells called monocytes	3. Chemotherapy are the white blood cells good or bad?

Quote or word from article	Question
1. p.62 dendritic cells	1. Do dendritic cells make up dendrites?
2.	2. Aren't white blood cells bad?
3. Antigens	3. Are antigens the by product of dendritic cells?

"Teens' actions questioned after death at a party"

Quote from article	Connection to Quote
1. ...No, no, no, no	1. When people drink the lose good judgement
2. ...not in my car	2. Some people love "things" better than people or doing the right thing
3.	3.

Quote or word from article	Question
1. ...cops coming and seeing all the alcohol.	1. Why didn't they get rid of it? Or take the kid to the curb?
2. ...parentless beer party	2. Are the parents in trouble?
3. ...wealthy section of Harrison	3. Do rich kids kid preferential treatment?

"Lessons From the Crash of 1929"

Quote from article	Connection to Quote
1. ...1932 nearly 1 in 4 Amer. were unemployed	1. Hoovervilles - my mom's story of depression. How can we avoid that?
2.	2.
3.	3.

Quote or word from article	Question
1. ...secretly working to enrich themselves	1. Were people doing that before the crash of '29?
2. ...rotten experiences ...are great teachers	2. What did we learn from this latest crash?
3. ...interest rates are low	3. Can interest rates remain low? Should the be lower? How does this impact inflation?

article about dendrites and the immune system. The second one was done in a health/P.E. class. Students read a newspaper article about a teen party where illegal drinking was taking place. The third article was used in a business class, and students were using a history text to compare the crash of 1929 with today's economy.

Quad-Entry Diary

This is an example from an integrated algebra class designed for juniors and seniors who are not necessarily going on to additional math course work. Tay, the math teacher, adapted the double-entry diary to meet his instructional needs. The following example was used as a review for a chapter test. Students were

Figure 6.8 Algebra Quad-Entry Diary

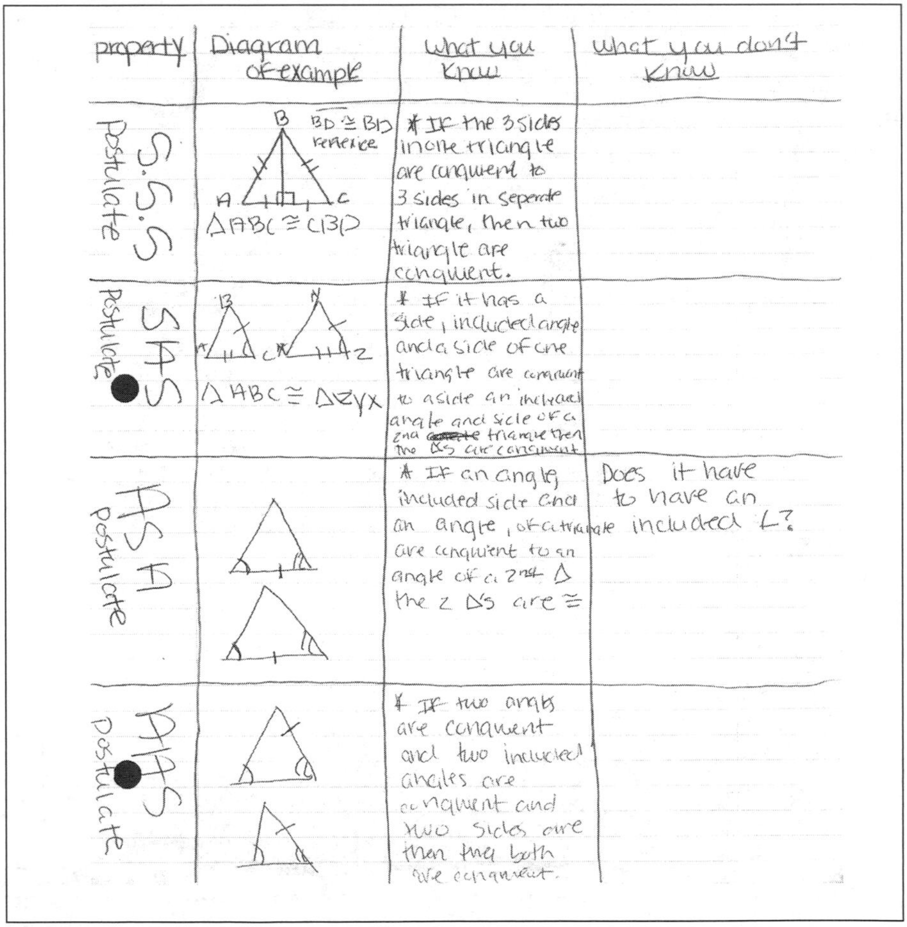

required to list four properties and write about each one. They needed to draw a diagram to represent each example and jot down what they thought they knew about each property. If they had a question, they could write it in the last box (see Figure 6.8).

Toward the end of the period, Tay gave the students an opportunity to ask their questions. The questions guided the review and helped clear up any misconceptions. Tay could see where the gaps to his instruction were and reteach parts that were unclear.

Integrating Notes and Comprehension Constructors

By the middle of the semester, students can often choose which tools to use with different reading tasks. As I look at my own processes as a reader, I realize that sometimes I can't make a connection because I need more background knowledge. If that is the only way I am allowed to respond, I can't respond at all. In this situation, what I really need to be doing is asking questions so that I can build more connections. When there are several ways to respond to the text, the student as well as the teacher tends to get more out of the exercise.

For this reason, I have become less prescriptive. I am more concerned that students have a variety of options they can use as they think about text.

For example, college preparatory English 12 students are reading *The Sunflower* by Simon Wiesenthal. The author grapples with forgiving a German officer after the Holocaust, and the book includes more than fifty brief commentaries by a wide range of people considering his choice. The text is dense, and the content is complex. If students are going to understand this piece in a meaningful way, they need opportunities to talk about their reading. Before they can talk, they have to have read the material and record some thinking.

In the first example, Kim has turned in sticky notes from her reading (Figure 6.9). She has removed the sticky notes from her book and recorded the page number on each one. Because she has shown me some of her thinking, I can better see how to guide her learning.

Her reading assignment is in twenty-five-page increments. As she read, she jotted down ten different places where she demonstrated thinking. Reading her examples, I can tell that she is asking questions that don't have simple answers. Perhaps her group can help her draw some conclusions. She asks what a *coup de grace* is. I can answer that one for her. Kim is connecting to characters, which helps her understand or disagree with their actions. She is drawing conclusions on her own based on her connections and what she has learned from the book. I can see that Kim is thinking.

Emily decides that she wants to demonstrate her thinking by using a double-entry diary (Figure 6.10). For her, this tool works better. She records her lifted

Figure 6.9 *The Sunflower* Notes

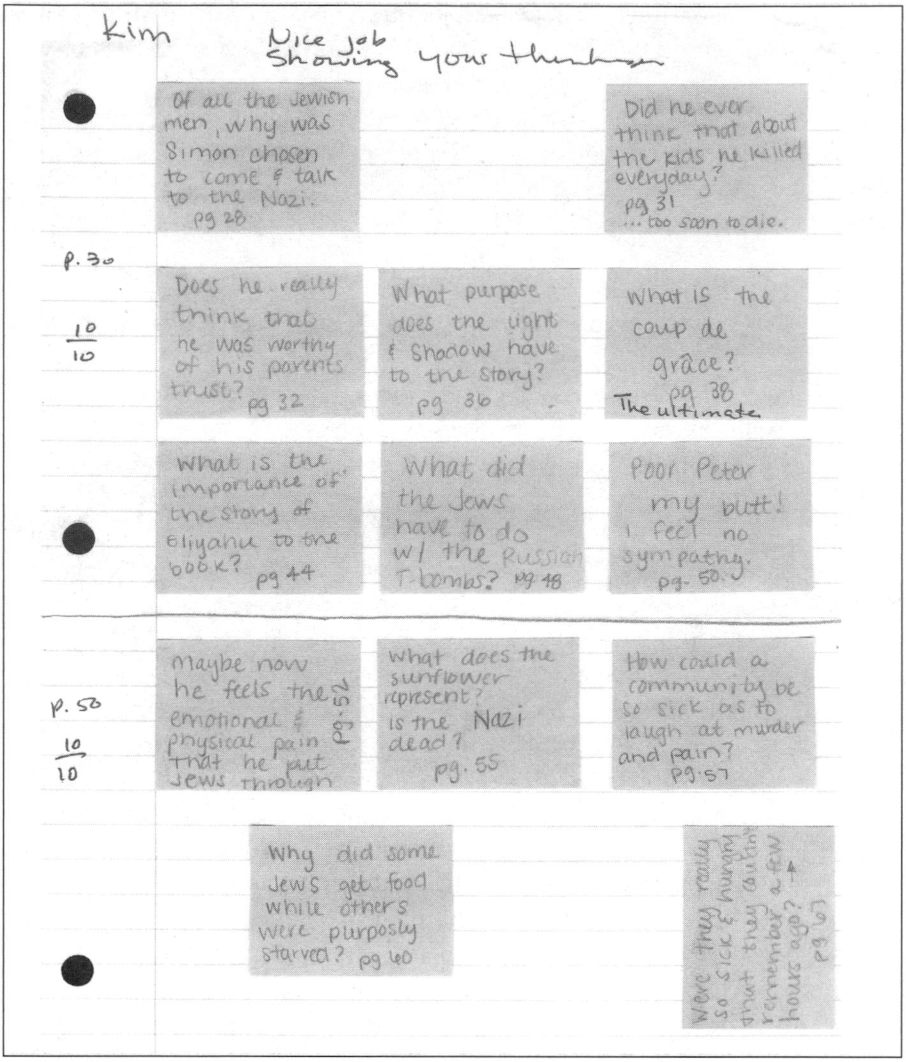

quotes from the text in the boxes on the left. On the right-hand side are boxes that Emily uses to record her thinking about the quotes she has chosen.

The last example is a copy of a transparency that contains "group thought" (Figure 6.11). I once saw a poster in a middle school classroom that read, "Individually we are smart. Collectively, we are brilliant." All readers can benefit from the talk of others, so I have students work individually, knowing they will have the support of the group and can try out ideas with others. They also know

Figure 6.10 *The Sunflower* Connector

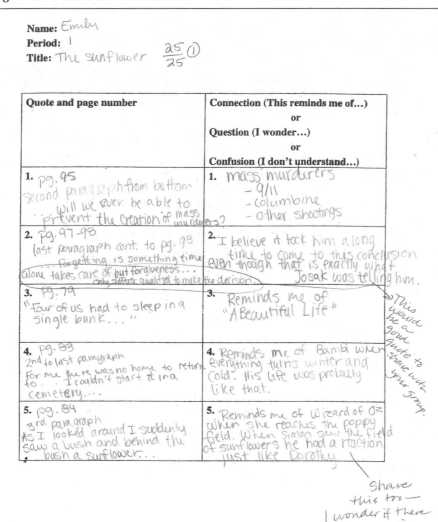

that group time isn't a "free-for-all." I will be holding them accountable. I will collect and give points for their group tool. However, the biggest motivator is sharing the group tool as an overhead with their peers.

The sticky notes and marking text allow me to hold students accountable for the reading. I can also hold groups accountable for their work, asking them to record their thinking on a group double-entry diary.

Figure 6.11 *The Sunflower* Group Notes

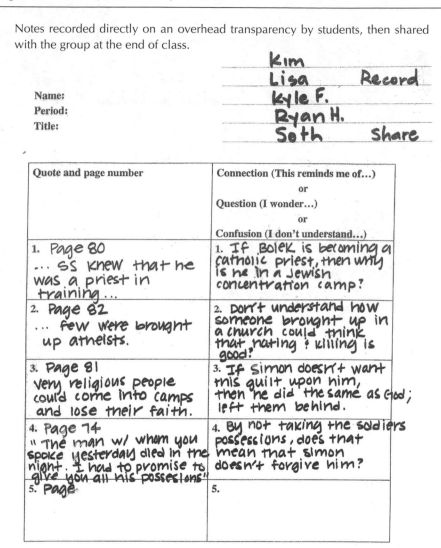

Notes recorded directly on an overhead transparency by students, then shared with the group at the end of class.

Kim
Lisa   Record
Kyle F.
Ryan H.
Seth   Share

Name:
Period:
Title:

Quote and page number	Connection (This reminds me of...) or Question (I wonder...) or Confusion (I don't understand...)
1. Page 80 ... SS knew that he was a priest in training ...	1. If Bolek is becoming a catholic priest, then why is he in a Jewish concentration camp?
2. Page 82 ... few were brought up atheists.	2. Don't understand how someone brought up in a church could think that hating & killing is good?
3. Page 81 Very religious people could come into camps and lose their faith.	3. If Simon doesn't want this guilt upon him, then he did the same as God; left them behind.
4. Page 74 "The man w/ whom you spoke yesterday died in the night. I had to promise to give you all his possesions"	4. By not taking the soldiers possessions, does that mean that simon doesn't forgive him?
5. Page	5.

What Works

1. Give students something to look for and write as they read. Model different ways that readers mark text and hold their thinking while they read.

   Teaching point: Good readers trust the author and their own abilities as readers. They don't panic if at first the text doesn't make sense—they trust that there are clues in the text that will help their understanding.

2. Show students how to use a double-entry diary (see Chapter 2). Throughout the year, you can provide different options with these diaries for marking thinking. This tool is especially helpful when reading nonfiction text.

   Teaching point: Good readers know there are different ways to mark text while reading. When one tool isn't working, they can easily select another that may be more helpful.

3. Share with your students what you do to help yourself remember what you read. Perhaps you write in the margins; maybe you jot notes to yourself. Notice what you do as an expert reader of your content to set a purpose, and share that with your students.

   Teaching Point: Good readers rely on experts to show them how to negotiate unfamiliar text. Let them see how you ask questions, adjust your reading rate, and note your thinking so that you can return to it later.

7

Group Work That Grows Understanding

Curriculum is often thought of as a set of specific knowledge, skills or books to be covered. I propose instead that we think of curriculum as a set of important conversations that we want students to engage in.

Arthur Applebee

I scan the room to see who needs my help. I'm pleased to report that no one does. Groups are completing the assignment I've designed to help them build background knowledge of recent wars. Each group is assigned a different war to research: World War II, the Korean War, the Vietnam War, the first Gulf War. We have been reading news articles about our country's ongoing involvement in the Middle East, and they need to understand some of the history of U.S. military conflicts to interpret current events.

Students are in groups of five or six. A giant tablet of chart paper and colorful markers burden one person's desk in each group as he or she records the group's ideas. Each group member seems to be poring over a variety of accessible text. Everywhere I look, students are reading, writing, and talking together.

One group moves back and forth between the U.S. history text and a recent article from *Time* magazine. Another group is discussing an editorial from the *Denver Post* questioning the buildup of troops on the Kuwait border. Megan's group is reading sections of *The Sunflower* and discussing how the moral conflicts in this book about the Holocaust are similar in some ways to today's conflict in the Middle East.

Kyle's group is reading an article about the Korean War given to me by a teacher in the history department. I overhear him say, "Have you noticed how all of these recent wars connect? Like, this war with Iraq and Vietnam. I don't think people who lived during the Vietnam War wanted it to happen either."

Corrie agrees, "Yeah, I'm amazed that a president would just do something that the American people didn't want, like go to war."

"I thought Congress had to declare war," says Nicole.

"Not in this case," replies Josh. "They just called it a police action."

"What's the difference between a police action and a war?" wonders Corrie.

"I wondered that too," says Chris. "Maybe we should read with that question in mind."

My role during discussion groups has changed in the last few years. I used to run around the room, like the plate spinner at the state fair, trying to keep everyone on task. Many times group work was just too exhausting to do on a regular basis.

I was tempted to give up on group work altogether a few years ago, but I kept reading professional material that explained the benefits of small-group instruction and discussion. I decided I needed to figure out how to make groups work.

There is an art to discussion, and people can get better at it if they have timely feedback. My students appreciate that I point out to them what they are doing well. They need to know what is working so they can continue to do it. Students also try to implement my suggestions to improve their group work. Then I can help them figure out how to fix what isn't working.

Why Small Groups?

I am often asked by high school teachers how they are supposed to teach their content and reading when they have classes of thirty or more filled with such a wide range of readers. It is typical for secondary teachers to have struggling readers, excellent readers, and everyone in between, all at the same time. I know the answer from personal experience. But because the answer is difficult to implement, I'm always afraid to share it. The answer is small, flexible groups.

Why Do I Ask Students to Discuss Reading in Small Groups?

Discussion . . .

stimulates higher levels of thinking,
develops social skills,
develops listening skills,
encourages articulation of thinking,
honors all learners,
holds kids accountable,
helps students remember,
allows students to make connections,
allows others to see different perspectives,
    and
promotes deeper understanding.

I have always been pretty good at holding the entire class's attention. My problem with groups for years was management. When I first began using groups, I made a major mistake. I would say to kids, "Okay, now get into groups and talk about what you've read." It was chaos.

I was trying to control every group, but because I couldn't be with every group at once, many of them were off task. If I wanted the class to function during group time, I had to share the responsibility with my students. If I didn't want to be in charge of every group's thinking, I had to show students how to work without me.

I began doing a little research and decided I needed to observe small-group settings with experienced, competent group members. I observed my book club, watching other adults talk and listen. I watched teachers at department meetings. I visited first-grade classrooms and watched kids work where teachers such as Debbie Miller (2002), author of *Reading with Meaning,* had prepared them for groups. I began to notice patterns. There were observable behaviors that determined how well the groups functioned.

Questions arose that I needed to think about if I wanted groups to work in my classroom. For example, how does a group work successfully with someone who monopolizes the conversation? What does the group need to do to make sure everyone's voice is heard? How do people in the group hold their thinking when they read, so that they remember what to talk about in groups? Is a facilitator necessary, and if so, what is his or her role?

After observing groups of adults that worked well, I was able to draw some conclusions about what needed to be in place for a group to function. We needed some norms. If the students were going to honor these norms, they needed to set them up themselves.

I started with a class of students in reading workshop at the beginning of the school year. Since they hadn't started meeting in groups yet, I asked the kids to remember their previous group experiences and jot down three things that really bugged them about working in groups. This was easy for them. Even though they relished the opportunity to complain, it was obvious that the majority of their complaints came from not having control over group work.

As I read the students' concerns, I had to decide what was negotiable and what wasn't. I categorized student complaints into three areas, and then added an action that would give students some control. I shared these common concerns and potential actions with the class on an overhead:

1. I hate being in a group without my friends. I don't like being with people who annoy me. (Adults feel much the same way, but they have a bit more control in deciding with whom they'll work. I wanted to have some say, forming groups some of the time, but I wanted them to feel like they had some control as well.)
   Student Action: If I am in a group that doesn't work for me, I will tough it out and request a different group next time.
   Teacher Action: I agree to honor group requests as best I can. However, as the person responsible for classroom instruction, I get the final say about group composition.

2. I don't like being in a group in which some people slack off and don't do their share of the work. I don't like it when some people talk all the time and don't get their work done. (There are few things worse than being in a group with people who don't do their share of the work. It's doubly

hard to get the work done when the people in the group are being distracting by talking and goofing around.)

Student Action: I recognize that I can't force anyone but myself to do something, and I agree to do my part.

Teacher Action: I won't expect students to police each other's behavior. I won't give group grades. Instead I will notice who is contributing and who isn't, and respond accordingly.

3. I don't like being in a group when I don't know what to do and no one will help me. (Being asked to do something without any help is frustrating and a waste of time. There needs to be support systems in place where people can get help.)

Student Action: I will help members of my group if I can. If I am the one who is stuck, I will ask my group members to help me first. If that doesn't work, I will seek help elsewhere—through the teacher, another group, or a text resource.

Teacher Action: I will model how the group is supposed to do something. I will also observe groups and share what is going well and what isn't working, in order to help groups run smoothly. I will be available whenever possible to answer questions.

What Interferes with Group Work?

• Someone hasn't read the material or completed the task.

Suggestion: This person goes to a designated quiet spot to finish the reading and writing before he or she joins the group. If the whole class hasn't read the assignment, maybe the text is too hard, or maybe class time needs to be used for silent reading before discussion groups can meet.

• Someone talks all the time.

Suggestion: Give this person a job. Have the student record thoughts on a chart or in a group double-entry diary. Provide some words that other group members could use to politely remind the culprit that he or she is monopolizing the conversation. For example, "Great idea, _____. I wonder if you could let someone else respond." Or "Thanks for your thinking, _____. I wonder what _____ has to say."

• Someone doesn't talk.

Suggestion: I think it is okay to honor someone's decision to listen. It is important, though, that this person have a chance to be heard. Sometimes people don't talk because they don't want to break in and seem rude. Use prompts such as "_____, you haven't said much. Would you like to add any thinking to the group?"

We talked about these norms as a class, tweaked a few parts, and then voted. Everyone in the classroom had to either agree to the norms or make a suggestion that would improve them. Everyone agreed to try the norms. The next step was showing them what I wanted to see in groups.

I decided to invite my friend and colleague Chryse Hutchins into my classroom to help me demonstrate ways to talk about reading. Chryse suggested that we do something called a fishbowl in front of the class. She explained that we would sit in front of the students, modeling what we wanted them to see, while they watched and then talked about what they saw.

I liked the idea and decided to design a sheet that would guide student observations and help the kids remember what they observed. I asked Chryse to mark the novel she had brought with a few sticky notes and jot down some thinking on each one. Little did she know that she would be modeling the "good" behaviors of a group member while I demonstrated some not-so-good behaviors that I had observed.

The next morning I introduced Chryse. We put the students in a circle and began. Chryse had her book and sticky notes. She asked if I wanted to share first, but because I didn't have my book, I responded, "No, you go ahead." I noticed some students writing on their observation sheet. They noticed that not only did I not have any thinking marked on sticky notes, but I didn't even have my book with me.

Chryse began with a quick overview of what she had read so far. I listened until she started sharing her sticky notes. I then turned my back to her and started a conversation with a student behind me.

Chryse stopped. She was catching on that she was the good student and I was the distracted one. She waited for me to finish. I could see more students writing. Surely they were documenting my rudeness. Chryse asked me if there was anything I wanted to know about her book. I said, "No."

She said, "Then why don't you share something from your book?"

"Well, I don't have my book, so I can't share any specific part, but I can share a connection." I briefly mentioned a connection. Chryse talked about my connection, and we decided the students had seen enough for one day.

The students noticed several behaviors (see Figure 7.1). They saw the importance of bringing the reading material to a group. They saw how having thinking held on sticky notes could drive the discussion. They saw how deadly it is to a conversation to lose eye contact with the speaker. They observed how rude it is to interrupt talking or even worse, not respond to a question. They saw that connections and questions were ways to jump-start a stalled conversation. Overall, they saw several behaviors (good and bad) that could occur in a small group.

Rehearsal for the Big Show

Writing assignments are always better when group work is done beforehand. Group discussions give students an opportunity to rehearse and construct connections before they sit down to that daunting blank screen or piece of paper. Small-group settings also allow me to meet more of the individual needs in my classroom. I can group struggling readers together for a while and help them with a decoding strategy. I can then change their group and let them be part of another group that is having an in-depth conversation about the topic.

I start at the simplest level with groups, by providing everyone in the class with the same image or piece of text. One fall in reading workshop, I put up a cover from *Time* magazine labeled "Ticking Time Bomb." It was a stick of dynamite with a lighted fuse, highlighting a feature on terrorism cells within the mag-

Figure 7.1 Student Fishbowl Notes

> **What did you notice about the fishbowl conversation?**
> They tell and answer and talk back and forth.
> They both had eye contact.
>
> **What did Chryse and Mrs. Tovani share?**
> What happened (summary) in their book.
> Opinions about the books.
> Chryse tells how she thinks (journal)
> where the book takes place.
>
> **How could you tell they were listening to each other?**
> They asked questions about the book that
> they want to know about the other book.
> Using everyday life to connect to the book.
>
> **What did Chryse and Mrs. Tovani do well?**
> Talked to each other about the book
> and feel what each other feels.
> Having different opinions about a
> character.
> Refere to other books.
>
> **What could Chryse and Mrs. Tovani have done better?**
> Mrs. Tovani could of asked more questions
> that she wanted to know about the
> book when Chryse was talking about her
> book. She looked like she was bored.
> You looked at us and not at chryse.
>
> **What will you try when you share your book?**
> Ask questions that I have about the
> book.
> What happened so far in the book.
> How I feel about the book.
> Make a connection.

azine. Each student had one sticky note on his or her desk. They had to write one thought about the cover on their sticky note. Groups of six to eight students then had to combine the comments on one sheet of paper, read them together as a group, and look for connections between the comments. This activity doesn't take long, and it's a good way to introduce some of the core ideas of group work—everyone must do some prep work and share it with others (see Figure 7.2).

Figure 7.2 Sticky Note Comments for Group

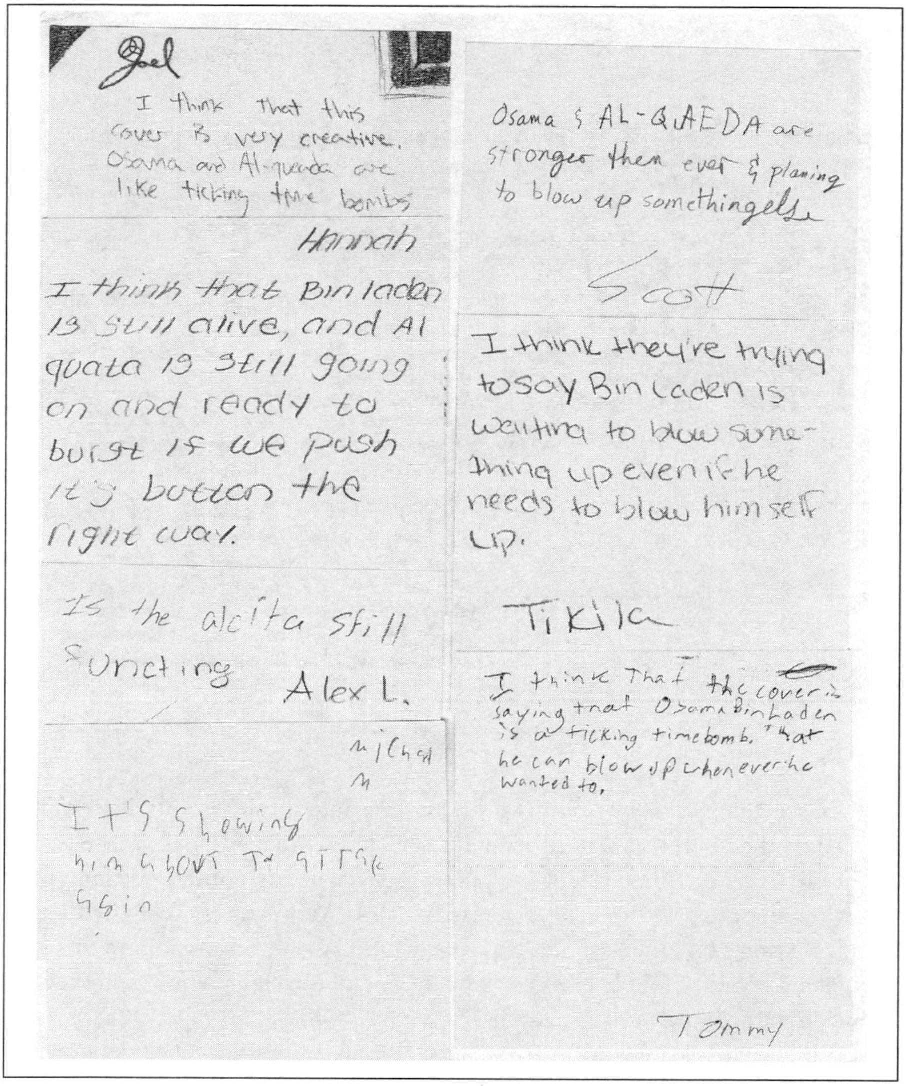

Eventually students move into more sophisticated records of their group conversations. I often use the Highlight and Revisit comprehension constructor in groups (see Figure 7.3). A blank copy of the comprehension constructor is in the appendix. Students read and highlight individually a short piece of text I've given to everyone in the class. In groups, they write down in the first column the exact words highlighted by someone in the group, reasons for the highlighting, and the deeper thinking that comes from considering the quote.

Figure 7.3 Highlight and Revisit

Quote Highlighted (record words from text)	Reason for Highlighting	New or Deeper Thinking
1. He envies people who live in their own time.	What does this mean? Are there really people like this? Question	Does time repeat? Could this be a metaphor of some sort?
2. In this world, time is like a flow of water occasionally displaced by a bit of debris, a passing breeze.	Plot, setting, around ocean, spring early fall maybe summer a day	People are sometimes afraid of change so they stay the same way their whole life and never improve.
3. They are not questioned about coming events about future marriages, births..... left alone & pitied	What does this mean? Are there people that hate changes?	Some people are afraid to make changes because they don't want to change the perfect future they have in their mind. They won't try anything fun or different. They want to be alone.
4.		
5.		It's like a picture of the ocean. Tim thought it is a metaphor for the people that are afraid of changes. Like the seasons change. It sounds that it is spring and someone is near the ocean staring at it.

This activity usually results in students seeing similar points being highlighted by their peers, as well as some unique choices that spark new discussion.

I often ask one member of the group to serve as a recorder, putting group notes on chart paper or overhead transparencies. We might end class with each group sharing a bit of these notes with the whole class for discussion. In this way, students are leading whole-class work by the end of the class period, and they see connections across group discussions.

While students are working in groups, I circulate around the room, noticing what is happening. I look for things that are going well, and I look for trouble spots. I use a standard form to take notes during groups, and I often share these notes with the groups and the whole class (see Figure 7.4). A blank copy is in the appendix. In the middle column, I write direct quotes from the group. I use the plus (+) column to write down behaviors that I notice help the group function. I use the minus (-) column for suggestions to improve the discussion.

Initially the comments on the positive side aren't as numerous as the comments on the negative side. At first I am looking for simple things such as the following: Are students facing each other? Does each person have his or her reading material, and a pen or pencil? Has thinking been held with a sticky note, marked

Figure 7.4 Group Observation Form

+	Reader's Quotes	−
Read from text then asked a question	Michelle said, "How do you rank powers?" Mike said, "Where does this knowledge come from?"	Group was having a hard time discussing certain aspects of the piece because they needed a working definition of terms: soul, senses, higher/lower powers.
Isolated confusion	Niki said, "I can understand this part but not that part."	
	Calysta said, "Is there a connection to time in a biological sense? Offspring coming back? Food chain—plants reproduce so higher powers can live. It's like the circle of life."	
	Lincoln said, "Life is repeating itself in order to preserve life." Calysta said, "That's why you don't want drilling in the Arctic. You want oil for your grandkids."	Discussion needs to go to the application of learning. What's the so what?
	Brianna said to Hillarie, "There you go!" Tyler smiled and nodded, "Yes."	What do you do when the thinking and talking stops? How do you go deeper?
	Lauren said, "I have no thinking. It turned off."	How do you bring someone back to the group?

text, a double-entry diary, or a comprehension constructor? By sharing suggestions of what can be improved, I soon begin to see more sophisticated behaviors.

For example, over time I notice that students not only have their reading material, but are citing textual evidence. After a few weeks, I notice that they are listening more closely to their group members, as well as acknowledging their thinking by asking a question or sharing additional thoughts. They seem to raise the standard of their talk because they want to be quoted in my notes and during debriefing sessions. Students feel comfortable with pauses, and return to their notes to continue the discussion.

I can't expect students to get better at discussion if I don't give them specific and immediate feedback. The observation sheets also help me decide where to go

Guiding Students in Groups

1. Suggestions for sharing what we've read:
   a. Give an overview of what's been read so far.
   b. Share something interesting from the book. For example:
      A character action
      An opinion about something that's happened
      A question
      A provocative part
      A confusing part
2. Suggestions for writing a better response:
   a. Share your thinking about a quote.
   b. Consider questions that don't have simple answers.
   c. Ask your group members their opinion.
   d. Ask yourself, "Am I just retelling, or sharing my thinking?"
   e. Make a statement or recommendation, and use textual evidence to support your thinking.

next with my instruction, and spark thinking about my role in groups.

Group work is challenging. Groups don't always work and that can be frustrating. It's tempting to go back to whole-group instruction because it is so easy to control. When group work gets me down, I have to remember its benefits. I also have to remember the message I am sending to kids about the importance of working with others. Harvey Daniels (Daniels, Bizar, and Zemelman 2001) writes about the benefits of group work this way:

When we ask students to sit in rows, or when we discourage the sharing of work, we send a very different message than when we have students sit at tables and solve problems together. Students who are given opportunities to collaborate every day receive the loud and clear signal that working and thinking with others is an important skill, valued both in school and in the real world. (p. 157)

Talk helps all learners articulate their thinking. Small groups also give more students a chance to participate in a way that they wouldn't do in large groups. I am often amazed by the thinking that comes from small-group settings.

What Works

1. Show kids how to discuss. Use real-world examples. Let them know that a multitude of responses can be acceptable. Help them see different options for sharing thinking.

   Teaching point: Good readers use talk and collaboration with peers to extend their thinking about text.

2. Give students specific feedback: Debrief with them what you notice about their discussions. Share what students did well, and let them know how they could improve. Capture their quotes whenever possible. Begin with short periods of discussion followed by immediate feedback. Increase discussion time as students improve.

Teaching point: Good readers improve the way they talk and listen to peers when given specific feedback. They use observations of both strengths and weaknesses to inform their work with peers.

3. Use powerful pieces: No one wants to discuss something dull. Pieces that lend themselves to controversy also work well. Many times short, provocative pieces encourage students to read and discuss.

   Teaching Point: Good readers talk about their reading to solidify their thinking. They don't waste their time talking about text that doesn't generate interest or differing opinions.

4. Anticipate stumbling blocks: Think about adult groups. What do you do when one person talks all the time? How can all the voices in the group be heard? How can a group be brought back on track? How can new thinking be generated?

   Teaching Point: Good readers know that group dynamics can either help or hinder the talk that takes place. If norms aren't established and honored, the group disintegrates. Change the makeup of the groups every so often to ensure that students' interest levels, social levels, and skill levels are met as they shift over time.

Group Management Questions

How do you know when groups are finished?

Students are finished when they feel confident enough to move on to more reading and writing about the topic. In my class, an assignment is usually attached to the group work. Sometimes students write an essay after a discussion group or have another reading assignment or project to complete. If students think no more talk is needed, they move on to the next task.

How do you get the talking going again when you come to a stalled group?

Ask a question of the group or pull out a specific line that strikes you. Ask them for their opinion. Share thinking that has been held in a double-entry diary or a sticky note.

8

"What Do I Do with All These Sticky Notes?" Assessment That Drives Instruction

The hardest part about reading is remembering what I've read.

Jessica, ninth grader

What's up?" A senior nods as he recognizes a familiar face. His friend motions him to sit at a desk next to him, near the window. More brand-new seniors enter the room, trying out their new status as the top dogs. It's the first day of school, and everyone has their "cool" face on. You know the look: it's the one where they try to hide their excitement that summer is over. No one is smiling or talking. They merely nod their heads at peers, strolling into the room with their hands in their pockets, or arms hugging fresh notebooks.

The bell rings and I begin. "Welcome to College Prep English 12. This year we are going to spend a lot of time together learning about reading, writing, and thinking. I hope by the end of the semester you will become extremely selfish."

I pause. A few students look at each other and shrug. A boy who has just walked in and has heard only the part about becoming selfish says, "No problem there. My mom tells me I'm the most selfish person she knows."

I smile. "Good. You are ahead of the game." I continue on. "Make sure you get something out of this class every day. Before you read anything, I want you to ask yourself, 'What's in it for me?' Don't read for your teacher or your parents or your friends. Read, write, and think for yourself." No one says a word. They look at me with big eyes, not sure if they can trust me. Curious to hear their thinking, I ask, "Are there any questions?"

"What about tests?" asks a big kid in the back.

"Yeah, what about tests?" asks another student.

Not the question I was looking for, but at least it gives me some insight into what they care about. "What about them?"

"Are we going to have a lot of tests?'

"It depends on how you define tests," I answer.

"You know. Tests. You give us something to write about and we try to figure out what you want." A few kids snicker, thinking I've just been burned by this exchange. But the student who first asked the question continues, and I can see that he's not being disrespectful. "I'm not very good at taking tests. They're usually worth a lot of points and kids like me don't do very good on 'em." It's obvious he's trying to decide whether he should drop the class and find an easier one.

"That's a good question. I can see that you're concerned about how I will grade." I decide to skip what I had planned to launch the class and answer their questions about tests.

I begin by saying that we each have a job to do. "My job," I say, "is to show you how to think about your reading and writing. Your job is to show me that you are thinking." I go on to explain that there are many different ways that a student can show me what they know. They may be used to showing what they know by taking tests and quizzes or by writing papers and answering questions. This class will be different, I say, and there are many other ways to show thinking besides taking a test. I mention sticky notes and text marking, double-entry diaries and comprehension constructors. I explain that these tools will help them not only demonstrate what they know, but also remember what they've read.

I continue by telling them that for me, measuring their thinking will be ongoing, and that we won't have a test on something and then never talk about it again. I won't expect students to read my mind. I will be explicit about what they need to know, because school should not be a game of "let's see who the teacher can trick."

"So we're like going to have tests every day?" queries a girl in the front with a nervous smile.

"In a way we will, because every day you're going to be expected to think and share that thinking. But the good news is, I'm not looking for one right answer. There will be lots of possible answers. It will be hard for you to fail if you are willing to share your thinking."

Teachers Care About Tests, Too

Students aren't the only ones who want to know about assessments and tests. Teachers are curious too. They want to know about the way I measure and grade. More important, they want to know how I can tell if my students are improving as readers.

When it comes to assessment, I am a selfish teacher. I want to assess my students' thinking in a way that informs my teaching. I used to think that I didn't do much assessment in my classroom. I always associated assessment with traditional tests—especially tests that were long, complicated, and disconnected from what was actually being done in the classroom. Our students have to take some tests like that, but I prided myself on not being a teacher who gave them.

I never really liked the word *assessment* until I realized that without assessment I cannot inform my instruction. I agree with Grant Wiggins (1998) when he writes "The aim of assessment is primarily to educate and improve student performance, not merely to *audit* it" (p. 7).

Now I realize I am assessing students all the time, every day in my classroom. I try to guide my assessment by considering a few questions.

> **Questions to Drive My Instruction**
>
> 1. What do the strategies look like as a student's thinking becomes more sophisticated?
> 2. How do the strategies connect to real-world learning, and how do students use the strategies outside my class?
> 3. How do I know when a student is ready to have a new strategy introduced?
> 4. How do the strategies connect to other strategies?

It's important that my assessments be ongoing and purposeful, useful to students as well as to me. I should be able to tell students what they are doing well and what they need to improve upon with each assessment. This means I give students multiple opportunities to demonstrate thinking. I don't want a student's final attempt at a task to be a failure. Rarely do I give students a poor grade if they are willing to try again. I want kids to take risks and try again, because that's the only way they are going to get better at reading and writing. Many unsuccessful high schoolers come to ninth grade with multiple Fs from middle school. They just didn't do the work. Many times they didn't do the work because they didn't know how. Any teenager would rather be perceived as lazy than stupid.

Assessing in Context, Strategy by Strategy

I used to secretly hope that I could find one perfect assessment that would tell me all I needed to know. It was a sad day when I realized there would never be one single measurement. I had to decide what I wanted to measure and then find or design the assessment.

I recently examined the standardized assessments given by local school districts, and there were plenty. The majority of assessments were used to inform the way programs were being used. Some measured how well one English department did compared with another. Other tests gave reading levels based on arbitrary measures. When I asked who used the information, I was told, "Classroom teachers."

As a classroom teacher, I can say that districtwide and statewide assessments are not very helpful. In reality, these tests are much more useful to real estate agents who are trying to sell homes in the "nice" part of town. These assessments aren't helpful to me, because they rarely inform daily instruction.

One-shot assessments such as chapter tests don't help me teach. They measure finite knowledge, but don't give any information about the way students think. And they don't help students see how they can use the new knowledge. David Perkins (1992) writes about the limits of what he calls inert knowledge:

> *Startlingly often, students have knowledge that they remember when directly quizzed, but do not use otherwise. It doesn't come to mind in more authentically open-ended situations of need, such as writing an essay, pondering the morning's headlines, considering alternative professions, selecting a new stereo, or for that matter, studying another subject. Knowledge of this sort is called inert. As the phrase suggests, inert knowledge is the knowledge equivalent of a couch potato: It's there, but it doesn't move around much or do anything. (p. 22)*

If teachers want students to comprehend and actually use content from their classrooms, they need to show them how to be better thinkers about that content. A science teacher who wants to help students read, write, and think like a scientist has to have insight into the students' thinking processes, not just what they know about mitosis. In Dennie Palmer Wolf's book, *Reading Reconsidered,* she writes, "Thoughtful reading is only rarely a matter of flashy insight. More often it is a gradual, groping process" (1995, p. 31). Meaning does not arrive. It is constructed over a period of time.

There are strong assessment implications in these statements. When I am assessing students, I look at the ways they are using strategies. It doesn't matter if I am talking with them during a quick conference, or listening to them in a small-group discussion, or reading their writing. I am looking for evidence of their thinking. Figure 8.1 includes some questions that I use to assess students' thinking in different strategic contexts.

Starting Points: Goal Setting and Whole-Class Charts

I know of no single measurement that is sophisticated enough to demonstrate proficiencies of the goals in Figure 8.1. Because of this, I use multiple assessments.

We begin in many classes with simple goal setting. At the beginning of the quarter, we brainstorm possible reading and writing goals, and each student chooses one. Throughout the quarter, we revisit the goals individually and collectively, adapting them where necessary. At the end of the quarter, the students and I decide whether the goals have been met. If not, what prevented students from doing so? It's okay if students want to stick with their first-quarter goal after they discuss it with me.

Potential student goals might include the following:

Figure 8.1 Assessing Strategy Use

Activation of Background Knowledge
Can students access existing information to make connections between new and known information? Is there evidence that making connections helps students to
    relate to the subject matter in a way that enhances interest and deepens understanding?
    visualize in a way that helps students remember what is being read?
    ask questions that can lead to a deeper understanding?
    use background knowledge to interpret textual evidence?
    draw inferences based on personal experience and knowledge?
    determine importance based on personal experience and knowledge?
    clear confusion and repair meaning by connecting new information to the known?

Student Questioning of the Text
Can students ask useful and authentic questions about the text in a way that enhances understanding and encourages deeper understanding? Is there evidence that asking questions helps students
    build background knowledge about an unknown topic?
    answer questions by drawing conclusions beyond the unseen text?
    isolate confusion by asking a specific question of someone who is more knowledgeable?
    read on to quell curiosity?

Drawing Conclusions and Making Inferences
Can students combine their background knowledge with textual evidence to draw logical conclusions? Is there evidence that drawing conclusions helps students to
    think beyond the literal meaning to the unseen text?
    use existing knowledge and textual clues to support inferential thinking?

Monitoring Comprehension and Using Fix-Up Strategies
Can students recognize signals that indicate they are confused? Do students have strategies that repair meaning? Is there evidence that monitoring comprehension and using fix-up strategies helps students to
    identify confusion?
    recognize that several strategies can be used to repair meaning?
    apply appropriate strategies that repair meaning?
    recognize that rereading with a different purpose in mind can improve comprehension?
    adapt strategies to meet the demands of the text and the purpose of the reading?
    recognize that subsequent reads yield deeper levels of comprehension?

Determining Importance in Text
Can students identify different purposes for reading? Do students recognize unique features of texts, author styles, and similarities in topical information to distinguish important ideas from interesting details? Do students recognize that purpose determines what is important? Is there evidence that determining importance in text helps students to
    recognize that purpose is used to sift and sort important information?
    isolate important ideas from lesser details?
    recognize organizational features in text to aid comprehension?
    recognize unique features of an author's style?
    use background knowledge to interpret importance?
    ask questions to build background knowledge so importance can be established?

Finishing a book more than 150 pages long

Reading a new genre

Learning two new strategies to keep the mind from wandering while completing a dull text

Learning how to pick out a good book

Figuring out what to do when encountering unknown words

We work on collective charts as a class, parallel to these individual goals. These ongoing assessments of our work in learning new strategies remain on the walls and show collective changes in thinking over time.

I start a chart at the beginning of the year that can help students assess and redefine reading. Figure 8.2 is an example of one such chart I recently completed with a group of reading workshop students. Stopping every few weeks to add to the chart reminded students of the ways they could use the strategies we'd been exploring in the previous weeks.

Conversation Calendars

I work with teenagers because I enjoy them and am fascinated by their lives. Conversation calendars help me know them as people, so that I can assess what they need as learners. In *Rethinking High School*, Harvey Daniels (Daniels, Bizar, and Zemelman 2001) and his colleagues encourage us to have a broader view of adolescence:

> *In popular culture, adolescence is routinely depicted as a wholly negative time, a stretch of misery, a struggle and a curse. Those of us who work with teenagers every day reject this toxic stereotype. Of course, these years can be hard, damn hard, even heartbreaking at times. But adolescence is also suffused with amazing, joyful, exhilarating possibilities: deep friendship, powerful emotion, reaching toward the new, trying on and discarding possible identities, coming into possession of your powers as a physical body and a thinking person. And let's not forget music and laughter and dancing and, maybe, falling in love a time or two. (p. 22)*

I see my students in these words. It is difficult for me to assess students' reading needs if I don't know them. Conversation calendars help me learn about my students' lives outside the classroom. I then have the background knowledge I need for conversations that allow me to discover their strengths and passions. Once I know what they care about, I can help them see how the work we are doing in class is purposeful and connects to their lives.

Figure 8.2 Redefining Reading Over Time

On August 30 we knew how to help ourselves make sense of text by
- visualizing a picture in our heads;
- rereading a portion of the text;
- slowing down our reading rate;
- underlining a capitalized name so we pay more attention to it;
- talking to other readers to see what they think about the pieces.

On October 2 we added more ways to help ourselves make sense of text by
- asking questions while reading;
- making connections to things we already knew: experiences, TV, movies, other reading;
- using a purpose to sift and sort factual information;
- drawing conclusions: "Reading books like we read people";
- wondering about something, then using connections to help answer the question.

On November 13 we added more ways to help ourselves make sense of text by
- setting a purpose:
  —making connections to something that we know about in our lives. This helps us relate and learn something new versus just memorizing it.
  —revisiting difficult parts of text and reading them with a different purpose in mind.
  —asking questions before, during, and after our reading.
- identifying confusion:
  —recognizing when there are a lot of unknown words.
  —recognizing when it is difficult to make comparisons and contrasts.
  —recognizing when it is difficult to retell what has been read.
  —recognizing when our minds are wandering.
- finding answers to questions:
  —going back and rereading with the question in mind.
  —going back to another resource.
  —asking the teacher questions.
  —asking a specific question instead of saying "I don't get it."
- thinking about specific questions that force us to consider the author's intent:
  —when was the piece written?
  —what do we know about the author's background?
  —what emotion do we feel when we read the piece?
  —how are text features used to demonstrate emphasis?

Conversation calendars also give me an opportunity to touch base with every student every day. Here's how they work:

The top row of boxes are a place for the students to write. Each day they write to me about something. I don't tell them what to write, but I do give them options. They can tell me something about themselves, or they can ask me something about myself. Perhaps they have a question they didn't want to ask in front of the class. Sometimes the calendars are a place to vent or think on paper. Often they are a place for a quick chat.

Making the Grade

Reading Workshop Class
Total Points for Semester: 2,000
Calendars:
     10 weeks, 100 points a week   1,000
Whole-Class Demonstration Work: 500
Individual Reading Assignments: 500

CP English (College-Bound Seniors)
Total Points for the Semester: 2,200
Response Logs:
     10 weeks, 60 points a week   600
Vocabulary Notebooks:
     10 weeks, 50 points a week   500
Vocabulary Quizzes:
     10 weeks, 50 points a week   500
Whole-Class Demonstration Work: 200
Discussion Group Work: 200
Essays: 2 @ 100 points   200

In the small box in the right-hand corner, students give themselves points. They can earn anywhere from zero to twenty points. If students have an unexcused absence, they earn a zero. If they come to class, participate, and act civil for the majority of the class, they earn twenty points. Each day I read their comments and quickly respond in the bottom box. The small box at the bottom of my half is where I assign daily points. At the end of the week, I total the points and put the number in my grade book. Seldom does my point total vary from the student's assessment. (For more on how I allocate points for grades, see the box.)

Figure 8.3 shows a calendar from Talea, early in the year. I learn from this conversation calendar that Talea is shy, and that she might not want to share her thinking yet. I will have to give Talea other opportunities and ways to show her thinking. I also learn that Talea values books and literacy when she writes that "books may make a change on the way you act." I know I can recommend a book that is more than a swift-moving plot that Talea might enjoy.

Often in my responses I ask questions about the way students read. For example, I might ask, "What strategies do you use to help yourself get unstuck?" or "What is hard for you when it comes to reading?" The answers often inform the way I teach because they help me know what to model.

Perhaps a social studies teacher will ask the kids to summarize what they learned at the end of the day. A science teacher may want students to record questions they have, or what causes them to wonder. Math teachers may want to explore how students perceive the use of mathematics in the real world. They may want to ask kids to make connections between the current math curriculum and how it will serve them outside of class.

Here are some tips for making calendars work:

- Have a tray in the room where calendars go every day. Explain to students that the calendars don't leave the room. Many times students will "accidentally" put the calendar in their backpack and then accuse the teacher of losing it. If students think the calendars never leave the room, they are much more willing to recheck their belongings.
- Respond daily. If I don't respond daily, students don't value the calendars and then they stop writing. Responding daily gives the teacher important information about the students' affect. It also allows students to see that the teacher cares about them and is interested in their lives outside of school.

Figure 8.3 Sample Calendar from Talea

MONDAY	TUESDAY	WEDNESDAY	THURSDAY	FRIDAY
Is there going to be a lot of presentations in front of the class? Write your points here. 14	I'm glad I stayed here because of the English credit, so after this year I think I'll have 3 English credits. 20	Did you say we didn't have to be video taped in september? I don't like to be on camara. 14	I have a niece that's 4 yrs old. She can be fun, but dont listen at times. 18	I think if you read and find a good book it may make a change on the way you act, and it might be a good influence on you. I think many kids don't read, because it doesn't start out with action like a video game. 20
No- we will only do one presentation in front of the class. Don't be nervous. All you have to do is share your book. 20	Good for you! I'm glad you stayed here too. I could tell that first day you would be a cool kid to have in class. 20	No problem. We are only going to visit with the people in September. No videotaping. '20	My nephew is three. He is so cute but some- times he is wild. He has a mind of his own. 20	I think you are right. Have you found a book that has had a powerful influence on you? (100) 20

- Make the calendar worth doing. If I give the students only a few points for filling out the calendar, they won't value the time it takes to write. By giving students the opportunity to earn points for participating, I am honoring their attempts to work hard. I am also padding their grade. Many struggling readers have been labeled as failures since second grade. Failing one more time at reading isn't going to help them. By giving them points for participating, I don't have to lower my standards in other assignments that are more demanding.

- Decide how to manage lost calendars. Sometimes students lose their calendar or forget to turn it in, and they lose 100 points. Losing 100 points can crush their grade. When this happens in my class, I give students opportunities to make up the points by giving up a free period and coming into my room to read. This doesn't sound like much of a loss. But if a student is a struggling reader, giving up a free period with friends to read can be a big sacrifice.

- Consider who will use the calendar. I have found them useful in grades 6 through 10. I use the calendars with classes for struggling high school readers. I probably wouldn't use them in an English class for college-bound seniors.

If I team taught at the middle school level, I would have a different teacher use the calendars each week. In other words, I would have the language arts teacher do it one week, the science teacher the next, the math teacher after that, and so on. If students filled out a calendar several times a day for several different teachers, it would lose its effectiveness.

- Experiment and vary the use of the calendar. I don't tell kids what to write, because I want them to have the ownership and latitude to express whatever they want. Sometimes I write a question in my box on Monday that I want the students to answer by Friday. I don't use calendars every week of every school year. I start out with calendars during the first several weeks because they are such a good tool for assessing students' needs and interests as readers. But I always take a break from them around midterms, when more written work is coming in. I do calendars about five weeks of every quarter during the year.

Reading Response Logs

Another way to get to know students is through reading response logs. These response logs allow me to see what students are reading and thinking about with self-selected texts (not assigned reading). The logs allow students a place to practice and demonstrate their use of the strategies they are learning in class. It is also a place for me to assess their understanding of the strategies.

It is important that I show students samples of response logs. They need an idea of what a good one looks like. Sometimes I use a student's from a previous class or share a sample from my personal reading. Each student is responsible for bringing in a spiral notebook; a seventy-page spiral notebook is usually enough to get them through a semester. To get full credit they must complete the following:

Read twenty-five pages a week. Students earn a point per page. This doesn't sound like much reading—only five pages a day, with the weekends off. This is a reasonable request, one that most students can tackle easily. Yet some students struggle with it because their schedules are so full, so I also have to make the assignment worth their while. If students choose to read more, great! I want the assignment to be short because mine is one of six, sometimes seven classes that students take. If the reading assignment is too long, they are tempted to fake their way through it. I want to give them an opportunity to read something they enjoy, and I want to honor their time for reading by making the assignment manageable.

A template for reading response logs that I give to students to help them remember what they have to do each week is in the appendix.

As part of the reading log, students must summarize their reading in four to six sentences. I have read a lot of the books in my room, but there are also many I haven't read. I tell this to kids right at the start of the school year. I'm not going to be the reading policewoman. If they want to fake their way through the reading, they can go ahead and try. The next two parts of the assignment make cheating a bit difficult. The purpose of the summary is to give me a clue of what they read for the week. It also gives them practice summarizing their reading in a succinct manner. Students can earn ten points here for a short, well-written summary.

Then students respond to the reading. I encourage them to write at least twelve to fifteen sentences, having found that giving them an idea of how long each part is supposed to be provides a framework. I don't penalize kids if they are a few sentences short, especially if their writing is thoughtful and well done. Twelve to fifteen sentences is an arbitrary number, but it is important for students to see that the response is longer than the summary and that the content is different. Ideally they will show a range of responses. They may make a personal connection to the piece or ask a question that makes them want to read on. I encourage them to pull lines from the reading that intrigue them and then ask them to write why the line strikes them. I often see conclusions students draw about characters or plot. Many times this is the most interesting and informative part of the reading response log. It is here that I can see how students are using strategies to manipulate the way they think about text.

Finally, students attach five sticky notes in their logs that show they are practicing the strategy we are working on in class. For example, if we are working on identifying confusion, students pull five sticky notes from their reading that demonstrate places they are confused about. I push them to ask a question that isolates their confusion. This is worth another ten points. I usually give two points per sticky note, for a total of ten. At the end of each entry, I respond to what students have written. I often ask questions, make my own personal connections, and try to "talk back" to them in an authentic fashion.

For example, Kim writes in her log about the book *Like Water for Chocolate,* "Today, I read about a girl named Tita who starts life off at a disadvantage." Kim pulls a quote from the book and records it in her log. She copies a few sentences from it in her log: "How unfortunate that black holes in space had not yet been discovered, for then she might have understood the black hole in the center of her chest, infinite coldness flowing through it."

Kim then writes a bit about plot but quickly launches into her thoughts about the book. "I would not even know what to do if I was in Tita's place. At first I didn't understand why Tita was so sad but as I read, I cannot help but feel sympathy for Tita. I put myself in her position and it upsets me. I can better understand why she cries when her mother is not around. When her mother is there she pretends to be strong and keeps her head up. I think she is strong even though she is lonely and sad. I wonder why Tita doesn't run away with Pedro like Gertrudis did. I am sure it wouldn't be easy but love is stronger than the reasons Tita has for watching the love of her life form a family with someone else."

Kim's response shows me that she has not only read, but is able to think about her reading in various ways. First, Kim makes a connection to the character, trying to understand why she does what she does. Kim infers that Tita is strong, but she also demonstrates through her questions that she is confused about Tita's actions. I feel confident that Kim will keep reading because she wants to find out why Tita allows her love to leave.

Students who are struggling readers aren't initially expected to respond in the same way college-bound seniors are. I modify my reader response logs in reading workshop in such a way that students can demonstrate thinking but aren't put off because they view the writing part as cumbersome and too difficult. Sometimes I ask these students to stop five to ten minutes before the end of class to write in the reading response logs. I want them to write briefly about what they remember, and then write about any thinking they did while reading.

For example, Faraz is reading a book about Tupac Shakur called *Back in the Day* by Darrin Keith. He cites a quote that he has lifted from page 22 and responds to it. The next day he fills his page with questions. He wants to know why Tupac's mom didn't want Tupac to sign a record contract. He is also curious about her involvement with the Black Panthers. Faraz wants to know how long she was a Black Panther and what exactly the Black Panthers did?

Faraz's questions propel him to read on. He has made his thinking permanent by writing down his questions, and he has demonstrated that he knows how to ask questions to which he doesn't know the answer. Based on what Faraz has shown me, I can decide what I need to teach him next. I will need to teach Faraz where to find the answers to the questions he has asked. I also now know that Faraz is interested in learning more about the Black Panthers and that I can be on the lookout for text on this topic.

Sometimes I want to keep just a sample of their thinking in a file folder of work samples or portfolio. Reading response logs won't work in that case, so I adapt the assessment by giving students a silent reading response sheet, which is in the appendix.

Collecting Reading Response Logs

If you decide to use reading response logs on a regular basis, you will need to decide how to collect and assess them and respond to each student. This task can be daunting. If you don't plan well, many a weekend will be ruined. I used to collect reading response logs on Fridays. I would carry them out to my car, and there they would sit. All weekend I would dread grading them, and when Sunday night rolled around, they were still in my car. Monday morning would arrive right on schedule. I would carry the logs back into school and announce to my students that this week we would not be doing reading response logs. Grading thirty response logs at once was too much.

Students still turn in reading response logs weekly, but now I collect six a day. I look at my attendance sheet and assign the first six people to turn in logs on Monday. The next six students on the list turn their logs in on Tuesday, and so on. If students turn their logs in a day late, I still accept them, but I deduct some credit. I always accept late work for a deduction of points rather than no credit, because I know struggling students would rather not do the work at all than do it wrong and be humiliated. I know that the only way students will get better at reading, writing, and thinking is if they actually read, write, and think.

File Folder Collection of Work Samples

At the beginning of the year, I make a file folder for each student. Inside the folders I keep samples of their work that demonstrates thinking. I collect a sample of their writing at the beginning, middle, and end of the year. I collect samples of double-entry diaries, conversation calendars, and sticky notes. I also put in important information about standardized test scores from previous years, notes from home, and recommendations from previous teachers. I am selective about what goes in the folder. I don't want it to become a mishmash of random worksheets. Everything that goes in must give me another piece of the puzzle of who the student is. I use the folder as a way to demonstrate proficiency or recommend remediation.

Quick Conferences

Conferences are perhaps the best assessment tool I have. During conferences I gain information about how to immediately teach and guide my students. As a high school teacher, my conferences look a bit different from the ones I did as an elementary teacher. I confer on a daily basis in every class, even if it is only for a few minutes.

Sometimes I pull up a chair next to a kid and we talk about the reading. Other times, I move around the room quickly, noticing what students are doing. My purpose for quick conferring is to see who is understanding the reading and strategy task, and who isn't. I want to find my "shills," the students who understand what I am asking them to do and can be models for the rest of the class. Often when we come back together as a group, I'll say, "David, read what you wrote on the left-hand margin." David reads what he wrote, and I try to name what he has done well: "Did you see how David shared his opinion about the piece? That's something that good readers do. They aren't afraid to share what they think. They know that it is okay to have an opinion. As a matter of fact, good readers sometimes give themselves a purpose for the reading by telling themselves before they start that they are going to see if they agree or disagree with the author. Good job, David." David gets to be the expert, and I get the opportunity to teach something about the behaviors of successful readers.

I am also looking for students who don't begin the task I've put before the class. Oftentimes they aren't working because they aren't sure what I want them to do. Sometimes the piece is too hard for some kids to read but is packed with valuable content. I can't just let them sit there; I have to help them through the piece. Quick conferences allow me to read part of the piece to kids so they can participate in the discussions.

Testing What Students Know

I've helped students redefine assessment by giving them final examinations that test what they've learned about themselves as readers. For example, here are some sample questions from a final exam I gave to college-bound seniors a few years ago:

> **Sample Questions from Reading Final Exam**
> 1. Attached to this sheet is the definition of reading you wrote for me during the first week of the semester. Look at your definition, and think about all that you know about reading. Compare your new knowledge of reading with what you used to know.
> 2. Define metacognition. Why is it important? Give a real-world example of metacognition. Be specific and thorough in explaining your example.
> 3. You are reading a very difficult text, one that doesn't make sense on a first read. List at least five strategies you could employ to help you understand the reading.
> 4. You are reading a difficult textbook. You have little background knowledge about the topic. Answer the following:
>   a. How do you know you are confused? (List five signals that indicate confusion.)
>   b. List two strategies you could use to keep your mind from wandering. Explain how each strategy will help you construct meaning.
>   c. List five strategies you could use to fix up meaning.

Assessment for me is about showing kids how to recognize when they are confused and when they are understanding text. I give them opportunities to earn credit by sharing that thinking.

In our profession, we've come to believe that assessment is about giving credit for the right answer. If we're looking only for the right answer, then students often will not risk admitting confusion. That really puts us teachers at a disadvantage, because then we have to play the role of mind reader. Without the assessments that can guide us, we have to guess where to go next in our teaching. It's so much easier if we can get students to share their thinking. That happens only when we tie their grades to the effort they put into getting that thinking about reading into written form, and into class discussions.

What Works

1. Decide what you want to assess. Give a variety of ways for students to demonstrate understanding. Base your assessments on what you value. One test won't measure everything.

    Teaching point: Good readers know there are many ways for them to demonstrate understanding. They recognize that not everything is equally important, so they give time and effort to what is valued.

2. Design assessments that are checkpoints for understanding. Because learning is an ongoing process, assessment should also be an ongoing piece of your classroom.

    Teaching point: Good readers know that learning never stops. They use assessment to inform and improve their performance.

3. Teach students how to use the assessment tool. Don't let format interfere with demonstration of knowledge.

    Teaching point: Good readers know that procedures are different from performance. If the way they are asked to demonstrate knowledge is too cumbersome, they will abandon the task.

9

"Did I Miss Anything? Did I Miss Everything?" Last Thoughts

If teachers become distant from their own learning they will most certainly become distant from the learning of their students.

Alisa Wills-Keely

It's eight o'clock Monday morning, and I'm already exhausted from the first-hour reading workshop class that didn't go particularly well. As students begin filing in for my second-hour reading class, I paste a smile on my face and try not to think of the weeks ahead. The state test is a month away, and I still have classes full of kids not progressing fast enough to do well on it.

A stack of mail is in my hand—I made a quick trip to the office between bells to pick it up. I sort through it as fast as I can, throwing all the advertisements and administrative memos I can avoid reading in the trash. The pile shrinks—I feel like at least I am accomplishing something before I have to start teaching again. A short handwritten message on a "While You Were Out" form catches my eye. I put it in the small "save" file to read later.

A disturbance in the back of the room draws my attention. I look up and see that Josh and David are slap boxing right next to Mike, who is already (and perpetually) asleep. I glance around the room and see the new student, Tanesha, nervously shifting in her chair. Her eyes widen as Ella barges in the door, crying. Ella announces to all who will listen that she's just been kicked out of her second foster home and is living with Ramon, the school drug dealer.

I glance down at the "While You Were Out" message and actually read it: "If you witnessed the urinating incident last week please write up a statement." (See Figure 9.1.)

Now, for the record: No urination incident occurred in my classroom. I knew nothing about the incident mentioned on the form. I found out later it happened in the parking lot outside my classroom window, and the administration was soliciting anyone who might have witnessed it.

Figure 9.1 While You Were Out Note

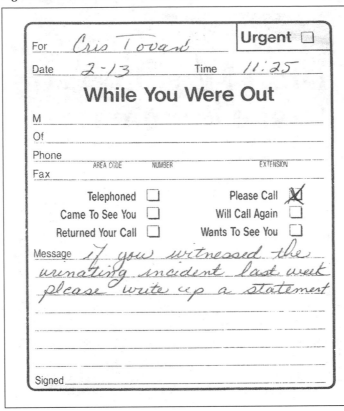

I've saved this small slip of paper for weeks in my files, amidst all the samples from kids who are making progress as readers in every content area. I want to remind myself how difficult it is to determine what is important when we are teaching. The constant and unexpected demands of this job stress us out. It's no wonder our students have trouble separating unimportant details from critical information when they are reading. Everyone faces this challenge throughout life, and we must take the same advice we give to students: focus on what is important and, as much as possible, ignore the rest.

Many times these decisions are made moment by moment, while we are reading or living our lives. Do I take the time to refer Josh and David for slap boxing, or do I quietly remind them that one more referral from any teacher will likely cause their expulsion? Do I spend the period cajoling Mike to wake up, or do I ignore him? Do I take the next step of calling his mom or checking with his caseworker to see if there is a legitimate reason for his sleepiness? Do I walk over to Tanesha and try to make her feel at home at this, her third high school in a year? Do I give Ella the acknowledgment she so desperately wants about her chaotic life outside school? Do I try my hand at writing in this new genre, the Urination Report? And do I have any time left to teach kids to read?

I can make good choices among all these options only when I have a clear purpose in mind. When it comes to teaching reading, my purpose can be informed by legitimate research and best instructional practices. Or it can be defined by other people's agendas. I can serve my students well only by reading, writing, and talking with colleagues. And most of all, I can never forget that in the midst of classroom upheaval, someone like Evan is always waiting to learn from me, and to teach me.

Rumor had it that the state test would include quite a bit of poetry this year, so I decided to give students a copy of a new poem each day and asked them to mark their thinking while reading with marginal notes. Evan was having none of it. Each day his work was sloppier and he put less time into it. Each day his copy of the poem was marked with few if any notes. Finally, on the day I handed out the poem "Did I Miss Anything?" (Wayman 1997), Evan exploded.

"Ms. Tovani, I have NO CLUE what this poem is about!"

"Evan, it's your job as a reader to find out what the poem is about. You can circle passages you like. You can ask questions. You can make connections to personal experiences. You can look at the title of the poem and keep it in mind as you read."

It's advice I've given him for weeks already, and I expect that it will have an effect on him sometime if I keep giving it to him.

That night, as I read Evan's marked-up copy of the poem, I see a reader (see Figure 9.2). He rereads the title before beginning each section of the poem, even marking each section of the poem with it to remember that strategy. He has a hunch that the teacher voice of the poem is sarcastic, which he confirms by the end of the poem. He even feels a little empathy with the teacher by the time he finishes when he writes, "Was he a teacher who had to put up with this question?"

He writes a brief note to me in the corner:

Dear Ms. Tovani:
Can I redo yesterday's work? I need to get an A. I am sorry that I drew all over and had illegible handwriting. Please?

I write a big "Yes" next to his request. Evan has discovered that a couple of the strategies we've used again and again in class really can work for him when it comes to making sense of poems. I see the first glimpse of a teenager who might someday be a confident reader. The final words of the poem touch me yet again, too:

Figure 9.2 Did I Miss Anything? Evan's Note

DID I MISS ANYTHING?

Question frequently asked by
students after missing a class

I asked this before each section after I read ~~it the~~ the poem after I did this it made perfect sense.

did i miss anything Nothing. When we realized you weren't here
we sat with our hands folded on our desks
in silence, for the full two hours

Is this the teachers responce? If it is is the teacher being sarcastic?

did I miss anything? –Everything. I gave an exam worth
40 per cent of the grade for this term
and assigned some reading due today
on which I'm about to hand out a quiz
worth 50 per cent

did I miss anything? Nothing. None of the content of this course
has value or meaning
Take as many days off as you like: *Being sarcastic? Yes!*
any activities we undertake as a class
I assure you will not matter either to you or me
and are without purpose

did I miss anything? –Everything. A few minutes after we began last time
a shaft of light descended and an angel
or other heavenly being appeared
and revealed to us what each woman or man must do
to attain divine wisdom in this life and
the hereafter
This is the last time the class will meet
before we disperse to bring this good news to all people
on earth

–is the author talking about students leaving college and teaching students of their children or even their jobs after school?

NW even though the teacher is being sarcastic.

did I miss anything? –Nothing. When you are not present
how could something significant occur?

did I miss anything? –Everything. Contained in this classroom
is a microcosm of human existence
assembled for you to query and examine and ponder
This is not the only place such an opportunity has been
gathered

what does this word mean?

Is the teacher saying that they are there for the question to learn and he didn't show up.

–but it was one place

–And you weren't here

do they mean that the student passed an opportunity to learn.

was he a teacher who had to put up w/ this question?

by Tom Wayman (originally from The Astonishing Weight of the Dead)

*Dear Mrs. Tovani,
Can I Re-do yesterday's work? I need to get an A. I am sorry that I drew all over and had illegible handwriting. Please?*

Yes!

Contained in this classroom
is a microcosm of human existence
assembled for you to query and examine and ponder
This is not the only place such an opportunity has been gathered
but it was one place

Our classrooms aren't the only place where kids might learn to "query and examine and ponder." But they are one place, and it matters that we see how important it is to offer students the opportunity again and again to take us up on the chance to think hard about the world around them.

We'll Never Have All the Answers

I think most of us become teachers because we love our content so much, whether it's poetry, quadratic equations, or the intricacies of cell formations or language construction. We love this content so much, we've dedicated the better part of our lives to teaching it to others. I don't see how we can be teachers of this content without spending at least some of our time with students helping them learn how to read about it.

When my first book came out, a friend told me she wrote a review of it on amazon.com. I was too embarrassed to tell her I had never even visited that site. That evening I went online and found her review. I kept reading and found another review, just after her kind words, from a teacher I didn't know. This reviewer wrote, "The criticism I have of Tovani's book is that I had hoped to find ready to use material for the classroom. Instead, I found that while reading it, the book forced me to re-evaluate my own instructional approach. Ultimately, this is probably a far better thing than any quick fix approach."

At first I felt a little guilty because I hadn't given this reader what she wanted. But then I was relieved that she thought it was a "far better thing" to have a thinking teacher in the classroom than a technician distributing worksheets. Teachers don't need any more canned programs or word-for-word scripts to "teacher-proof" their instruction. I didn't provide them in the first book, and you won't find them here.

It is presumptuous for me to think I know what's best for another teacher's classroom. It is my wish that teachers will take what is written in this book and adapt it to meet not only their needs, but the needs of their students.

One wizened veteran told me my first year that if I was going to be a truly great teacher, I would never be satisfied. No matter how confident or experienced I became, I would never be happy. She shook her head as she said, "Sadly, the good ones are always searching for better ways to teach children." She continued, "My wish for you is that each year you look back at your career and laugh with embarrassment about the way you used to teach. If you do this, you will continue to learn and grow."

When my first book came out, I was sure I would never have anything new to say about teaching reading. I was nervous, because I wondered what I would talk about when invited to work with groups of teachers. My friend and mentor Stephanie Harvey advised me, "Listen to teachers' questions. Don't dismiss them as unimportant. And never forget what it is like to be a teacher."

That's what I've tried to do. I still work with struggling readers, advanced readers, and every ability level in between, each morning in my classroom. I am spending more and more time each afternoon in science, math, history, and other classrooms where my students also work each day. Teaching adolescents to be better readers is no small feat. But we all know more about how to teach reading than we ever give ourselves credit for—we intuitively know our content and how to read it.

This book will help you in your teaching only if you trust yourself enough to listen to the voice inside your head that says, "I do know how to help these students become better readers. I do know what's important and worth my time, more than any published program or politician who hasn't been in a high school classroom since the day he graduated." This book has a few ideas that I hope can help you trust that voice. None of the activities are fancy or complicated. I hope that as you finish reading this book, you are saying to yourself, "I can do this." Sure you can. You know more about reading instruction than you think.

Appendix

Double-Entry Diary

Quote or description from a scene in the reading	Record of the strategy being taught

Comprehension Constructor with Connections Guide

Name: _____

Use a connection to the text to increase understanding.

1. Use your connection to make a statement about the text.

   Connection:

   So what?

   Statement about the text:

2. Use your connection to ask a question about the text.

   Connection:

   So what?

   Question about the text:

3. Use your connection to visualize a portion of the text.

   Connection:

   So what?

   Visual image:

4. Use your connection to relate to a character in the text.

   Connection:

   So what?

   What I understand better about_____.

"The Three Bears" Translation

Once upon a time was three bears: mama bear, papa bear, and baby bear. Live in the country near forest. NICE HOUSE. (No mortgage.) One day papa, mama, and baby go to the beach, only they forget to lock the door.

By and by comes Goldilocks. She got nothing to do but make trouble. She push all the food down the mouth; no leave crumb. Then she goes upstairs and sleeps in all the beds.

LAZY SLOB!

By and by comes home the three bears, all sunbrowned, and sand in shoes. They got no food; they got no beds. What are they going do to Goldilocks? Throw her in the street? Call a policeman?

FAT CHANCE!

They was Italian bears, and they sleep on the floor.

Goldilocks stay there three weeks; eating out of house and home; and just because they asked her to make the beds, she says "Go to hell," and run home crying to her mama, telling her what sons of bitches the three bears are.

What's the use? What are you going to do—go complain city hall?

Sample Text Set Guide Sheet

Title of Text Set: _____

Name: _____

Please complete the following tasks as you preview your text set:

1. Read one piece of text and answer the following questions:
Title:

Description of the piece:

One memorable aspect of the text:

2. Choose two other texts that look different from your first choice:
Title:

Topic:

Title:

Topic:

3. Write a letter to me addressing the following questions:
  a. What is your opinion of the contents of this text set?
  b. What should be added to make this text set better?
  c. How might you use this text set in U.S. history?

Instructional Purpose
(What Is Essential for Students to Know?)

1. What two places may cause students difficulty?

2. What will you model that will help students negotiate the difficult parts?

3. What do they need to do with the information they are reading?

4. How will they hold their thinking while they read?

My Answer Comprehension Constructor

Name: _____

Hour: _____

Question I asked that I can answer after reading the article:	Question my teacher could answer if I asked:	Question I can answer myself by inferring:
Question:	Question:	Question:
Answer:	Answer:	Answer:
Question I asked that I can answer after reading the article:	Question my teacher could answer if I asked:	Question I can answer myself by inferring:
Question:	Question:	Question:
Answer:	Answer:	Answer:

Template for Reading Response Logs

(Do not turn this sheet in. The information below should be copied into your reading response logs each week.)

Title: _____

Author: _____

Page _____ to page _____ = _____

Summary (4–6 sentences). Retell what you remember reading this week.

Response (12–15) sentences)

Possible ways to begin a response:
　　This connects to my life in this way . . .
　　I wonder . . .
　　This is important because . . .
　　I don't understand _____ because _____.
　　I want to remember this _____ because _____.
　　Quote a passage and then respond to it.
　　Record thinking that informs the way you want to live your life.

At the end of your response, include five sticky notes that demonstrate strategic thinking. Be sure the page number is written on each sticky note and adhere them to the page.

Points for each piece:
One point per page read, up to 25 pages
Ten points for a well-written summary
Fifteen points for a thoughtful response
Ten points for five sticky notes that demonstrate strategic thinking

Silent Reading Response Sheet

Name: _____

Hour: _____

Title: _____

Page _____ to page _____

While you are reading today, complete #1:

1. On the back of the page, share your thinking about what you read. You may want to tell about a confusing part and then try to ask a question that will isolate the confusion. Maybe you want to ask a question about something that you are just curious about. Share a line that strikes you or a personal connection that you make to the reading. Feel free to give your opinion or your assessment of the reading material. Your response should be at least five sentences long.

Before the class ends, spend five to ten minutes jotting down what you remember about today's reading. Try to write something that will jog your memory and help you remember where you left off. Stretch yourself to write more than you did the last time you did this sheet.

2.   I remember reading today about:

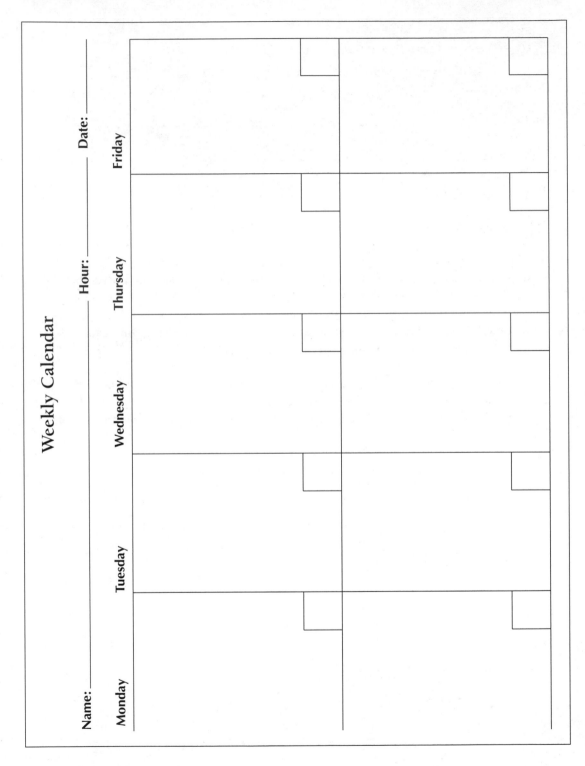

Weekly Calendar

Name: _____ Hour: _____ Date: _____

Monday	Tuesday	Wednesday	Thursday	Friday

Double-Strategy, Double-Entry Diary

Name:

Quote from article	Connection to quote

Quote or word from article	Question

Highlight and Revisit

Quote highlighted (record words from text)	Reason for highlighting	New or deeper thinking

Group Observation Form

+	Reader's Quotes	−

Bibliography

Allen, Janet. 2000. *Yellow Brick Roads: Shared and Guided Paths to Independent Reading 4–12*. Portland, ME: Stenhouse.

———. 2002. *On the Same Page: Shared Reading Beyond the Primary Grades.* Portland, ME: Stenhouse.

Allington, Richard. 2002a. "What I've Learned About Effective Reading Instruction from a Decade of Studying Exemplary Elementary Classroom Teachers." *Phi Delta Kappan* 83 (June): 740–747.

———. 2002b. "You Can't Learn Much from Books You Can't Read." *Educational Leadership* 60 (November): 37–43.

Applebee, Arthur. 2001. "Engaging Students in Disciplines of English: What Are Effective Schools Doing?" *English Journal* 91, 6: 30–37.

Bjorhovde, Gorm. October 28, 2002. Letter to the editor. *Time.*

Cisneros, Sandra. 1992. "Salvador, Late or Early." In *Woman Hollering Creek.* New York: Vintage Books.

Daniels, Harvey, Marilyn Bizar, and Steve Zemelman. 2001. *Rethinking High School: Best Practice in Teaching, Learning, and Leadership.* Portsmouth, NH: Heinemann.

Danielson, Stentor. 2002. "Shark Photo of the Year Is E-Mail Hoax." *National Geographic News* (August).

Davey, Beth. 1983. "Thinking Aloud: Modeling the Cognitive Processes of Reading Comprehension." *Journal of Reading* 27: 44–47.

D'Arcangelo, Marcia. 2002. "The Challenge of Content-Area Reading: A Conversation with Donna Ogle." *Educational Leadership* 60, 3: 12–15.

Darvin, Jacqueline. 2000. "Poetry Meets Plumbing: Teaching English in a Vocational Classroom." *English Journal* 89, 6: 59–65.

Dillulio, Dan. October 28, 2002. Letter to the editor. *Time.*

Duffy, Gerald. 2002. "A Cautionary Afterword." In Richard Allington and Peter Johnston, eds., *Reading to Learn: Lessons from Exemplary Fourth-Grade Classrooms.* New York: Guilford Press.

Ebbers, Margaretha. 2002. "Using Nonfiction Genres to Promote Science Practices." *Language Arts* 80, 1: 40–50.

Gallagher, Kelly. 2003. *Reading Reasons: Motivational Mini-Lessons for Middle and High School.* Portland, ME: Stenhouse.

Harvey, Stephanie, and Anne Goudvis. 2000. *Strategies That Work: Teaching Comprehension to Enhance Understanding.* Portland, ME: Stenhouse.

Hutchins, Chryse, and Susan Zimmerman. 2003. *Seven Keys to Comprehension: How to Help Your Kids Read It and Get It.* New York: Three Rivers Press.

Hyde, Arthur, and Marilyn Bizar. 1989. *Thinking in Context: Teaching Cognitive Processes Across the Curriculum.* White Plains, NY: Longman.

Ivey, Gail. 2002. "Getting Started: Manageable Practices." *Educational Leadership* 60, 3: 20–23.

Keene, Ellin, and Susan Zimmerman. 1997. *Mosaic of Thought: Teaching Comprehension in a Reader's Workshop.* Portsmouth, NH: Heinemann.

Lightman, Alan. 1994. *Einstein's Dreams.* New York: Warner Books.

Miller, Debbie. 2002. *Reading with Meaning: Teaching Comprehension in the Primary Grades.* Portland, ME: Stenhouse.

Moore, David, et al. 1986. *Developing Readers in the Content Areas, K–12.* White Plains, NY: Longman.

Olshan, Matthew. 2001. *Finn.* New York: Bancroft Press.

Paulsen, Gary. 1989. *The Winter Room.* New York: Orchard Books.

Pearson, P. David, L. R. Roehler, J. A. Dole, and G. G. Duffy. 1992. "Developing Expertise in Reading Comprehension." In S. Jay Samuels and Alan E. Farstrup, eds., *What Research Has to Say About Reading Instruction,* 2d ed. Newark, DE: International Reading Association.

Perkins, David. 1992. *Smart Schools: From Training Memories to Educating Minds.* New York: The Free Press.

Pressley, Michael, and Associates. 1990. *Cognitive Strategy Instruction That Really Improves Children's Academic Performance.* Cambridge, MA: Brookline Books.

Preston, Richard. 2002. *The Demon in the Freezer.* New York: Random House.

Rose, Mike. 1990. *Lives on the Boundary.* New York: Penguin Books.

Rubenstein, Rheta, Timothy Craine, and Thomas Butts. 2002. *Integrated Mathematics, Book 2.* Boston: McDougal Littell.

Shelley, Mary. 1963. *Frankenstein.* New York: Signet Classic Penguin Books.

Strong, Richard, Harvey Silver, Matthew Perini, and Gregory Tuculescu. 2002. *Reading for Academic Success.* Thousand Oaks, CA: Corwin.

Thomas, Marilyn, Charles McLaughlin, and Richard Smith. 2002. *Glencoe Physical Science.* Columbus, OH: Glencoe/McGraw-Hill.

Tovani, Cris. 2000. *I Read It, but I Don't Get It: Comprehension Strategies for Adolescent Readers.* Portland, ME: Stenhouse.

Vacca, Richard. 2002. "From Efficient Decoders to Strategic Readers." *Educational Leadership* 60, 3: 6–11.

———. 2003. Keynote Address. Annual Meeting of the International Reading Association. Orlando, Florida, May 5.

Wayman, Tom. 1997. "Did I Miss Anything?" In *I'll Be Right Back.* Toronto: Ontario Review Press.

Wiesenthal, Simon. 1997. *The Sunflower.* New York: Schocken Books.

Wiggins, Grant. 1998. *Educative Assessment: Designing Assessment to Inform and Improve Student Performance.* San Francisco: Josey-Bass.

Wolf, Dennie Palmer. 1995. *Reading Reconsidered: Literature and Literacy in High School.* New York: College Board Publications.